Bugsy

MALONE

THE PLAY

ALAN PARKER

D0302598

CollinsEducational

An imprint of HarperCollinsPublishers

Acknowledgements

Photographs on pages 72 and 74 by permission of Chris Ford, Keighley Youth Theatre. All other photographs, courtesy of Alan Parker, from the film *Bugsy Malone*.

Song Lyrics:

Bugsy Malone © 1975 Hobbitron Enterprises. Inc.
Fat Sam's Grand Slam © 1975 Hobbitron Enterprises, Inc.
Tomorrow © 1975 Hobbitron Enterprises, Inc.
Bad Guys' Song © 1975 Hobbitron Enterprises, Inc.
I'm Feeling Fine © 1975 Hobbitron Enterprises, Inc.
My Name is Tallulah © 1975 Hobbitron Enterprises, Inc.
So You Wanna Be a Boxer © 1975 Hobbitron Enterprises, Inc.
Ordinary Fool © 1975 Hobbitron Enterprises, Inc.
Down and Out © 1975 Hobbitron Enterprises, Inc.
You Give a Little Love © 1975 Hobbitron Enterprises, Inc.

ISBN 00 330230 X

CollinsEducational, London and Glasgow.
First published in 1984
Reprinted 1984, 1985, 1986, 1987 twice, 1989, 1990 twice, 1991, 1993

Typeset by Columns of Reading.
Made and printed in Great Britain by
Hartnolls Ltd, Bodmin, Cornwall

INTRODUCTION

It was back in 1973 that I originally had the idea for *Bugsy Malone*. To be perfectly fair, my eldest son had the idea – which I promptly pinched. The embryonic story and characters were then tried out on my four children during long drives to Derbyshire.

Raising money for the film was to prove more difficult than writing the script. I remember nervously sitting in many outer offices of the powers that be in Hollywood and Wardour Street. I'd clutch my script, my book of drawings, my test photographs and do my sales pitch to the patient moguls: 'Well, it's a gangster film . . . er, a musical . . . a sort of a pastiche on all the old Warner Brothers movies. . . . It's a world of would-be gangsters, showgirls and dreamers . . . er, except . . . (clear throat, look at shoes, shuffle papers) there're no adults in the cast, only children, average age about 12.' I saw a lot of expensive fillings in those days – in the gaping mouths of incredulous film executives. Most of them, I'm sure, thought I'd be more at home in a looney bin than on a sound stage at Pinewood Studios.

We managed to pay for the year-long preparation period with money my producer, Alan Marshall, and I earned from making television commercials. Every Bird's Eye beefburgers commercial we did paid for yet another poaching forray to New York, where I would stalk schools in Harlem, Brooklyn and the Bronx armed with one of the first 'portable' black and white video recorders. Back home our first priority was to look for American-speaking children at the various specialist schools and American Air Force bases all over Britain. We also began to check out the slightest rumour of a talented youngster in every dance school and theatrical group we could find. We did finally get the money to make the film, aided by the quick footwork of our friend David Puttnam, who is a wizard at performing the three card trick necessary to extract finance from film studios. David also promptly arranged my introduction to Paul Williams, whom I wanted to do the music. Our first meetings, in Las Vegas, were in between his twice nightly cabaret shows, when we would talk about the story and characters. 'Talk' is not quite the right word as Paul would croak in a low whisper to save his voice for the late show. Needless to say, we didn't get very far. By the third day we decided to have lunch to thrash it out. Four beef spitfires, two banana boozles and a great deal of Coors beer later, we had the structure for the basic score. Six weeks later we were rehearsing on Pinewood Studio's 'H' stage.

We had taped over a hundred different Christmas shows and dancing schools before we arrived at our chorus and for all the parts over the year we had auditioned over 10,000 children. Sifting through the 24 hours of video tapes and narrowing it down to the selected cast was a daunting task. Even more daunting was Alan Marshall's chore of telling the unsuccessful finalists (or worse still their mothers) that they weren't going to make it. Add to this, filming for 13 weeks, making over 300 specially cut-down costumes, designing a complete 1929 New York street set, setting up a full-time school for lessons in between scenes, finding ways of making the cars and splurge guns *nearly* work, getting child work permits from two countries and 33 different local councils and we were on our way. A thousand custard pies and 100 gallons of synthetic cream later we had our film.

As I write, *Bugsy Malone* has now been running in cinemas around the world and on television for eight years. The chorus, as far as I know, still plan to meet under the clock at Pinewood in ten years' time (two to go). One bike-mobile, I believe, still exists (just) and is occasionally wheeled out at Pinewood open-days like an old Spitfire.

In all this time I've had countless requests from schools and amateur dramatic groups for the script, so that they could mount their own productions. Fortunately I had written the novel of the film immediately after filming, so that helped a little, but, in the main, different teachers cobbled together their own scripts as best they could. Sometimes, I think, it was often a case of stop-framing the video in order to scribble down the lines and lyrics, and asking the music teachers to transcribe the music. What all this proved to me was that I should write a proper theatrical version that could be easily managed on stage without resorting to too many tricks – cinematic or theatrical. The version in this book has been written for production in the simplest sense and it can be elaborated upon as is thought necessary by the director, using the facilities he or she has available. Naturally, different productions will have their own strengths. For instance, in a school with a strong art and craft department, the sets can be made more elaborate. The same goes for costume, music and dance. I never fail to be astonished at the photographs I get sent from productions all over the world, and the ingenuity of the teachers and pupils involved.

The important thing, it seems to me, having seen many amateur productions, is for people to treat the play flexibly: to make the most of the individual strengths and talents of the children in their school or dramatic group and not to be restricted by trying to ape the movie. We've included comments from some of the teachers who have already put *Bugsy* on in their schools, to give a flavour of how problems can be solved. I wish you well.

In conclusion, I'd like to thank Jayne Potter of Collins Educational for her help with this book, Marion Dickens of Armada who published the original novel, Alan Marshall for his usual good sense, Keith Parker for the helpful suggestions on his school's production and Paul Williams for his lyrics . . . 'You give a little love and it all comes back to you'.

Alan Parker
Pinewood Studios, November 1983

ACT ONE

House lights on.
'BUGSY MALONE' played. Instrumental.
Black. Ominous piano music.
A red light flickers onto the dark stage. **Roxy Robinson** *enters along the audience gangway. Scared.*

BUGSY (*O.S.*)   Someone once said, if it was raining brains, Roxy Robinson wouldn't even get wet. In all of New York they didn't come much dumber than Roxy the Weasel. To be frank, Roxy was a dope.

Roxy *nervously runs right and left across the stage. Scared. O.S. we hear sound effects: screeching car tyres; slamming car doors; voices.*

BRONX CHARLIE (*O.S.*)   Shoulders, the alley-way quick. He's making for Perito's. Benny cover the back. Yonkers watch the sidewalk.

The **Hoods** *enter stage left:* **Bronx Charlie, Laughing Boy, Benny Lee,** *and* **Yonkers. Roxy** *is trapped.*

The **Hoods** *slowly walk towards him.* **Roxy** *backs away, taking off his hat. Impending disaster. Over this we hear:*

BUGSY (*O.S.*)   Dumb as Roxy was, he could smell trouble like other people could smell gas. But he should never have taken that blind alley by the side of Perito's Bakery.

BRONX CHARLIE   Your name Robinson?

ROXY   Uh huh (*Nods*)

BRONX CHARLIE   Roxy Robinson?

ROXY   Uh huh (*Nods*)

BRONX CHARLIE   Also known as Roxy the Weasel?

ROXY   Uh huh (*Nods*)

BRONX CHARLIE   The same Roxy the Weasel who works for Fat Sam?

ROXY   Uh huh (*Nods*)

1

Roxy *is splurged and the* **Hoods** *walk off. A jump and a click of the heels. Accompanying music.*

BUGSY (*O.S.*) Whatever game it was that everyone was playing, sure as eggs is eggs, Roxy Robinson had been well and truly scrambled.

Two **Undertakers** *walk on and carry off the stiffened body of* **Roxy**, *under their arms like a tailor's dummy. A* **Violinist** *playing a funeral melody walks behind them.*

Light up on **Barber** *cutting* **Flash Frankie's** *hair. Radio sound effects of a horse-race. Enter* **Bugsy** *stage right.*

BUGSY (*to audience*) Now, the guy in the chair here is Flash Frankie. The best lawyer in New York. Sure, he's a little shady, but he's the best . . . believe me, Flash Frankie's silver tongue can get a guy out of jail quicker than a truck load of dynamite. . . .

The **Hoods** *from previous scene again enter, dramatically.* **Flash Frankie** *is splurged, as is the* **Barber**. *The* **Undertakers** *move in, pick up the stiffened, splurged bodies and exit. They stop at* **Bugsy** *who reverently places a hot towel over* **Frankie's** *petrified face. The* **Violinist** *has been playing throughout and exits with the* **Undertakers**.

BUGSY Now, as you can see, something kind of fishy is going on here. To be perfectly honest, I'm beginning to wonder what's going on myself. . . . I mean this play's only just started and already the stage is full of stiffs! Oh, by the way, you're probably wondering who I am. My name's Malone, Bugsy Malone.

Light up on **Three Girl Singers** *left of stage, who sing into an old-fashioned microphone, the 'BUGSY MALONE' song which we hear under the subsequent action:*

Bugsy Malone

> He's a sinner
> Candy-coated
> For all his friends
> He always seems to be alone
> But they love him
> Bugsy Malone
> A city slicker

He can charm you
With a smile and a style all his own
Everybody loves that man
Bugsy Malone

Hot-headed Bugsy makes his mind up
Don't mess with Bugsy or you'll wind up
Wishing you'd left well enough alone
He's a man, a mountain
He's a rolling stone
And will he leave you
Sad and lonely, crying?
I couldn't say, but it's known
That everybody wants that man
Bugsy Malone

During the song, **Bugsy** *crosses right.* **Fizzy** *walks on, puts a chair on a raised box. A bookcase on wheels is pushed on, as is a counter, above which a sign reads:*

'BOOK EMPORIUM – A BOOK IS CHEAPER THAN A STEAK. READ ONE, LEARN A LITTLE AND EAT BETTER.'

Pop Becker *leans behind the counter.* **Fizzy** *gives* **Bugsy** *a shoe-shine throughout the scene.* **Bugsy** *reads his newspaper.*

Blousey *enters stage right, carrying a large bag with a base-ball bat protruding from it.* **Bugsy** *looks up from his newspaper and eyes her up and down.* **Blousey** *hands* **Pop Becker** *a piece of paper.* **Pop Becker** *knocks on the book-case. A door opens and he vanishes inside. Under the next lines we hear the* **Three Girls** *humming the 'BUGSY MALONE' song.*

BUGSY (*to audience*) With an Italian Mother and an Irish Father I'd naturally grown up a little confused. I didn't see much future as a spaghetti waiter at Mama Lugini's or pushing a pen at City Hall, so I'd drifted from this to that, you know, walking the line, trying hard not to fall either side . . . until, that is, the night I walked in here to Pop Becker's Book Store.

BUGSY (*to* **Blousey**) Hi, how you doing? I'm Bugsy Malone.

Blousey *ignores him.*

BUGSY You a dancer? A singer, right? Oh, a base-ball player.

He pulls her base-ball out of her bag.

BLOUSEY Zip the lip, wisey. I'm in no mood for conversation.

BUGSY You don't like me?

BLOUSEY Listen, wisey. I'm surprised you don't stoop with all that dandruff on your shoulders.

Bugsy self-consciously brushes his shoulders. **Pop Becker** *has returned through the book-case door.*

POP BECKER Honey, you can go in now.

Blousey steps through. **Fizzy,** *who follows her, speaks to* **Bugsy** *before ducking through the door.*

FIZZY If she's here about the audition, Bugsy, she's got a long wait. Every day they tell me to come back tomorrow.

BUGSY (*to audience*) Now, you might be wondering what kind of crazy place this is – with people disappearing into book-cases. Well, firstly, this neighbourhood ain't for dumb bums and secondly, this book store ain't no book store. This is Fat Sam's place – Fat Sam's Grand Slam – liveliest joint in town.

He pushes off the book shelves and the stage is lit fully for the first time. The 'BUGSY MALONE' song which has been playing continuously over the previous scene gives way to the loud and energetic 'FAT SAM'S GRAND SLAM' song. The stage is full and busy. The chorus dances.

Fat Sam's Grand Slam

> Anybody who is anybody
> Will soon walk through that door
> At Fat Sam's Grand Slam speakeasy
> Always able to find you a table
> There's room for just one more
> At Fat Sam's Grand Slam speakeasy
>
> *Once you get here
> Feel the good cheer
> Like they say in the poem
> Fat Sam's ain't humble
> But it's your home-sweet-home
> Plans are made here
> Games are played here
> I could write me a book

Each night astounds you
Rumours are a-buzzing
Stories by the dozen
Look around you cousin
At the news we're making here
Anybody who is anybody
Will soon walk through that door
At Fat Sam's Grand Slam speakeasy

See the politician
Sitting by the kitchen
Said he caught his fingers
In the well he was wishing in

Repeat

The number ends and we see **Bugsy** *and* **Blousey** *collide centre front of stage.*

BUGSY   Ouch, look where you're going will you.

Bugsy *rubs his shin.*

BLOUSEY   I'm sorry, I'm truly sorry. Oh it's you, Dandruff.

BUGSY   Don't worry, I've had a shampoo since we last spoke. That base-ball bat could be classified as a dangerous weapon you know.

BLOUSEY   My mother made me pack it.

BUGSY   You're a sports nut?

BLOUSEY   It's for protection, in case I get robbed.

BUGSY   You're a singer, right?

BLOUSEY   That depends on your taste in music. I'm here about a job.

BUGSY   Did you get the job?

BLOUSEY   They said come back tomorrow.

BUGSY   They always do. What's your name anyway?

BLOUSEY   Brown.

BUGSY   Sounds like a loaf of bread.

BLOUSEY   *Blousey* Brown.

BUGSY   Sounds like a stale loaf of bread.

BLOUSEY   Keep your jokes behind your teeth, wisey.

BUGSY   Pleased to meet you. I'm Bugsy Malone.

As they shake hands, suddenly we hear loud screams from the occupants of the speakeasy. The **Hoods** *from before burst in. There is full-scale panic. Tables are turned over; people run backwards and forwards across stage. Many people are splurged. The* **Hoods** *make their exit. One of the* **Hoods**, *an unfortunate called* **Doodle**, *drops one of the precious splurge guns. He runs out.* **Bronx Charlie** *sends him back for it.*

BRONX CHARLIE   The gun, Doodle! You dummy! Get the gun. You can't leave the gun!

Doodle *retrieves the gun, holding it the wrong way round so that he's pointing it at himself. He backs off, bumping into tables until* **Bronx Charlie** *and* **Yonkers** *return and physically yank him off the stage. The customers of the speakeasy pick themselves up and chat amongst themselves.* **Fat Sam** *appears from under a table. Nervously he tries to reassure his customers.*

FAT SAM   O.K. everybody, it's O.K., nothing to worry about now. Back to your tables. Razamataz! Music! I wanna see everybody enjoying themselves. Free drinks on the house. It's just a little excitement, that's all. No one can say Fat Sam's ain't the liveliest joint in town. (*Laughs nervously to himself*)

The band plays on, a little muted. **Fat Sam** *straightens a few up-turned chairs. He walks over to where* **Knuckles** *sits, propped up, holding his splurged arm. The other members of the gang are around him.* **Fat Sam** *touches the splurge. He examines the gooey mess on the end of his fingers.*

FAT SAM   Knuckles, dis means trouble.

Lights down to black. A paperboy runs through the audience waving newspapers and shouting excitedly.

PAPERBOY   Read all about it. New weapon for mobsters. Read all about it. New gang warfare flares. Read it in *The Record*. Read all about it.

On stage left a light on the **Radio Announcer**. *He reads the news bulletin with great urgency. The old fashioned microphone is as before. A large red 'ON AIR' sign now hangs behind.*

RADIO ANNOUNCER   We interrupt this programme of music to bring you an important news flash. . . . Reports are coming in of a gangland incident on the Lower East Side involving a certain Robert Robinson, known to the police as 'Roxy the Weasel', believed to be a member of the gang of alleged Mobster King, Fat Sam Stacetto. Robinson was the victim of a sensational event and we go over to our reporter on the spot for a . . . .

Light down on **Radio Announcer***. Light up on* **Fat Sam***'s room, on a raised platform right of stage.* **Fat Sam** *is ranting and raving. His trusted henchmen sit and listen intently.*

FAT SAM   So tell me how you allow this to happen? Roxy was one of my best. What have you got to say for yourselves, you bunch of dummies? Knuckles? Ritzy? Angelo? Snake Eyes? Call yourselves hoodlums. You're a disgrace to your profession. Do you hear me? A disgrace. And most of all you're a disgrace to me. Fat Sam.

He pats himself proudly. He goes to the drinks cabinet and gets out a glass and a decanter of orange juice. The gang are very dumb.

FAT SAM   And we all know who's behind all this, don't we?

GANG   Sure, Boss.

FAT SAM   You don't need a hatful of brains to know that, do you?

GANG   Certainly not, Boss.

They all shake their heads.

FAT SAM   We all know who's monkeying us around, don't we?

GANG   Sure do, Boss.

FAT SAM   So who is it, you dummies?

They look at one another, unsure whether they should answer.

GANG   Dandy Dan, Boss.

FAT SAM   Don't dare mention his name in this office.

Fat Sam *has fallen off his chair in excitement.* **Fizzy** *pokes his head around the door.*

FIZZY   Er Boss, er, how about my audition? You said come back tomorrow.

FAT SAM   Am I going mad? Are my ears playing tricks on me? Come back tomorrow, Fizzy.

FIZZY   But today is tomorrow, Mr Sam.

FAT SAM   Fizzy, will you get out of here?

Fat Sam lunges at Fizzy and in the process trips over Fizzy's bucket. Once again, the gang pick him up and brush him down.

LOUIS   You O.K. Boss?

SNAKE EYES   Take it easy Boss, you'll break something.

FAT SAM   Break something? Sure I'll break something, Snake Eyes. I'll break your dumb neck! Dancers, dancers. I'm surrounded by namby pamby dancers, singers, piano players, banjo players, tin whistle players, at a time when I need brains. You hear me? *Brains*! Brains and muscles.

GANG   You got us Boss.

Knuckles takes the soda syphon in order to top up Fat Sam's orange juice. Fat Sam holds out the glass. Knuckles squeezes and misses. The soda spray splashes everywhere but in the glass. Mostly, it goes on Fat Sam who is drenched and naturally furious.

FAT SAM   You! You manure face . . . you . . . you . . . great hunk of lard! Your trouble is you've got muscle where you ought to have brains. I tell you, my pet canary's got more brains than you! You dumb salami!

He pulls Knuckle's hat over his head. Snatching the soda syphon, he squirts it into Knuckle's face. Ritzy, Angelo, Louis, and Snake Eyes giggle. Their faces change as Fat Sam stalks them round the room.

FAT SAM   So what's funny?

He squirts the syphon at all of them.

GANG   Nothing Boss. Aaaaaaaah!

Light out on Fat Sam's office. Light up on Bugsy and Blousey who are left and front of stage. Bugsy is still trying to befriend her. She is still uninterested in him.

BUGSY   Can I give you a lift?

BLOUSEY   You got a car?

BUGSY Er, no.

BLOUSEY Then how you gonna give me a lift, Buster? Put me in an elevator?

BUGSY It's a nice night, we could walk. Which way you going?

BLOUSEY Which way *you* going?

BUGSY This way. (*Points left*)

BLOUSEY Then I'm going this way. (*Moves off right*)

BUGSY Let me carry your bag at least. Have you eaten?

BLOUSEY Ever since I was a child.

BUGSY Then how come you're so skinny smartie?

BLOUSEY I watch my weight.

BUGSY Yeah, I do that when I'm broke too. You hungry?

BLOUSEY No.

BUGSY You're not hungry?

BLOUSEY No, starving.

A table with a red check tablecloth has been brought on centre stage. A waiter holds the chair out for **Blousey** *to sit down. The* **Violinist** *walks on and plays his violin. The action is continuous, as is the dialogue. Other tables wih check cloths are brought on and people sit at them until a full restaurant is created. A surly waitress comes up, chewing gum. She is very bored as she waits.*

BUGSY Are you going back to the speakeasy tomorrow?

BLOUSEY Er no, I'm gonna try my luck at the Bijoux Theatre.

BUGSY The Lena Marelli Show?

BLOUSEY She's walked out. They're looking for a replacement.

BUGSY Oh, she walks out every week and every week they have auditions and every week she walks back again. . . . But don't let me put you off.

BLOUSEY You won't. What do *you* do?

BUGSY Oh, this and that.

BLOUSEY Oh, crooked huh . . . .

BUGSY No, not quite. I find fighters, boxers. In fact I was a fighter myself once, pretty good too.

BLOUSEY You were?

BUGSY Sure, I could have been a champion.

BLOUSEY You could?

BUGSY Sure, but for a couple of things.

BLOUSEY Like what?

BUGSY Like jelly legs, and a glass jaw.

BLOUSEY Some champion.

BUGSY I'd do well for a couple of rounds but I was about as tough as a ball of cotton wool. This jaw (*Points*) had more glass in it than Macy's window. One punch was enough to send me back to the dressing room – generally on a stretcher. . . . They'd slap my face, get out the smelling salts and I'd come round kidding myself it was a lucky punch. How many times can it be a lucky punch? Then I wised up, before my face looked like a plate of mashed potatoes. . . . (*He pushes his ear and nose to resemble a punched-up boxer.*) I could have been a contender, Charlie. (*Marlon Brando voice*)

Blousey *laughs.* **Bugsy** *kisses his fingers and touches her nose.*

WAITRESS (*chewing*) Look Buddy, in case you're wondering, I ain't part of the furniture. (*Pronounced 'foyniture'*) Are you eatin' or are you meetin'?

BUGSY Er . . . no, we'll have two Banana Boozles with double ice cream with nuts and chocolate sauce, two cream Arizona doughnuts and a coke with two straws.

Suddenly, there is pandemonium once more as the **Hoods** *rush in and splurge again.* **Bugsy** *and* **Blousey** *take refuge under the table.*

BUGSY We can't go on meeting like this.

They shuffle for safety, across the stage, on their knees.

Lights down. Lights up on **English Reporter** *in telephone box to the right of stage.*

ENGLISH REPORTER Now get this, news desk . . . there's been a frightfully bad show here in America chaps and this time the Yanks have gone too far and what's more it's just not cricket. And, as I speak, there's a pitch battle going on here and . . .

FOREIGN REPORTERS 1 AND 2 (*Similar to the above but in appropriate foreign languages.*)

Lights down to black. Much commotion. Lights up again and the three intrepid reporters are frozen by their phones, covered in splurge and custard pie.

Lights up on **Dandy Dan** *and* **Louella** *front of stage in their arm chairs.* **Dandy Dan** *in his silk dressing gown and cravat.* **Louella** *is elegantly dressed in satin. A* **Cellist** *plays next to them.* **Dandy Dan** *gets up and switches him/her off like a radio (by twitching the nose, perhaps).*

LOUELLA   Oh honey, don't switch that off, I was enjoying that.

DANDY DAN   I have to concentrate, Princess. I have a little business to attend to.

A **Butler** *has entered.*

BUTLER   I've shown Mr Bronx Charlie and Company into the conservatory, Sir.

LOUELLA   But ain't you gonna play no more, honey?

DANDY DAN   Later my rose, later.

He deftly kisses her hand and walks up the stairs to the platform on left. **Bronx Charlie** *and the* **Hoods** *jump up from their casual slumped positions, standing to attention, and yanking off their hats.* **Doodle** *is on the end of the line.*

DANDY DAN   Hi boys. O.K., relax. Well, guys, I'd like to take this opportunity of thanking you for your work so far. Everything's gone swell, just swell.

BRONX CHARLIE   Thanks Boss.

DANDY DAN   Fat Sam must have had quite a shock.

Dandy Dan *has taken five red roses and hands them out. He misses out* **Doodle**.

Bronx Charlie, Laughing Boy, Shoulders, Yonkers, Benny Lee, any moment now, Fat Sam will be crawling on his knees to me.

The **Butler** *walks on with a tray of custard pies.* **Doodle** *looks at his empty hand. There seems to be some mistake.*

DOODLE Er . . . I don't have a flower Boss.

Dandy Dan ignores him, takes a pie and hands the others to the other gang members.

DANDY DAN Soon all Fat Sam will have is the clothes he stands up in and a suitcase full of memories.

DOODLE Er . . . what about *my* flower Boss? I . . . don't . . . have . . . a flower . . .

Dandy Dan and the Hoods surround him.

DANDY DAN You goofed, Doodle. You dropped the gun. And I don't allow mistakes in this outfit, 'cause mistakes could put us all in the caboose and Sing Sing ain't my style.

DOODLE No Boss, please no. I didn't mean to drop the gun, honest I didn't. It just kind of slipped out of my hands. Any guy can make a mistake.

DANDY DAN Button your lip, Doodle . . . you're all washed up.

DOODLE Boss, give me a break. Boss!

They throw their pies at close range. **Doodle** *freezes and the* **Hoods** *carry off his stiff body. Lights down.*

Lights up on the opposite side of stage, front, where **Fizzy** *sweeps up. He whistles his song. The chorus girls,* **Tillie, Loretta, Dotty** *and* **Bangles,** *chatter away as they come down the stairs from* **Sam's** *office. Each one kisses* **Fizzy** *and leaves left of stage.*

TILLIE Night Fizzy.

FIZZY Night Miss Tillie. Night Miss Loretta.

Bangles gives him a huge hug and kiss, lifting him into the air, much to **Fizzy's** *pleasure.*

Night Miss Bangles . . . !

Fat Sam comes down the stairs, followed by the faithful **Knuckles,** *who cracks his knuckles as always.*

FAT SAM Stop crackin' your knuckles, Knuckles.

KNUCKLES But it's how I got my name Boss.

FAT SAM Well knock it off, or change your name. (*Calls up*)

Tallulah, are you ready? How much longer do you want us to wait?

TALLULAH (*O.S.*)   Coming honey. You don't want me looking a mess, do you?

Fat Sam *paces up and down nervsouly.* **Knuckles** *paces obediently after him.*

FIZZY   Er, Mr Sam, about my audition.

FAT SAM   Later Fizzy, I'm busy right now. Keep practising. . . . I'll see you tomorrow. . . . I promise you, tomorrow.

FIZZY   But yesterday you said tomorrow Boss.

Tallulah *has appeared, momentarily letting* **Sam** *off the hook.*

FAT SAM (*up to* **Tallulah**)   Tallulah! You spend more time prettying yourself up than there's time in the day.

TALLULAH   Listen, honey, if I didn't look this good, you wouldn't *give* me the time of day.

Fat Sam *storms off, frustrated* **Knuckles** *follows.*

FAT SAM   I'll see *you* in the car . . . (*to* **Knuckles**) Don't do that Knuckles.

KNUCKLES   Sorry Boss, it just slipped out.

TALLULAH   Night Fizzy. (*Kiss*)

FIZZY   Night Miss Tallulah.

Fizzy *is alone in the speakeasy. He sings (and dances also, if possible) his song.*

Tomorrow

> Tomorrow
> Tomorrow never comes
> What kind of a fool
> Do they take me for?
> Tomorrow
> A resting place for bums
> A trap set in the slums
> But I know the score
> I won't take no for an answer
> I was born to be a dancer now

Tomorrow
Tomorrow as they say
Another working day
And another chore
Tomorrow
An awful price to pay
I gave up yesterday
But they still want more
They are bound to compare me
To Fred Astaire when I'm done

*Anyone who feels the rhythm
Moving through 'em
Knows it's gonna do 'em good
To let the music burst out
When you feel assured
Let the people know it
Let your laughter loose
Until your scream
Becomes a love-shout

Tomorrow
Tomorrow's far away
Tomorrow as they say
Is reserved for dreams

Tomorrow
Tomorrow's looking grey
A playground always locked
Trains no winning team
I won't take no for an answer
I was born to be a dancer now

*Repeat

At the end of **Fizzy**'s *song, the curtain (if there is one) falls. If not lights to black.*

Curtains open. A lady in Viking helmet and breastplate comes from behind the join in the curtains and steps into a single spot. She clears her throat and starts to sing in a tortuous operatic voice.

SINGER   Velia, oh Velia the witch of the wood . . .

OSCAR DE VELT (*from the audience*)   Next!

SINGER   But I have other songs.

OSCAR DE VELT   Yeah honey, but do you have other

voices . . . ? Next. Come on, please, shake it up you guys, we've got a show to put on here.

Singer *leaves in tears.*

A magician in white tie, tails, topper and cape walks on centre stage.

MARBINI Good evening, I am the Great Marbini, Illusionist to Kings. I have been privileged to have obtained second billing at theatres in Missouri, Polar Bluff and Norfolk Nebraska, and I will now perform for you a trick seen before only by the crowned heads of Europe. From this hat, I will produce not *one* rabbit (*roll on drums*) not *two* rabbits (*drums*) but *three* rabbits.

OSCAR DE VELT Next! Next! Next! (As **Marbini** walks off) Don't give up your day job.

Light up on side of stage. A line of performers, all sorts and sizes, many exotically attired. **Bugsy** *and* **Blousey** *are among them.*

BLOUSEY I wish they'd hurry up. I get nervous waiting.

BUGSY Quit worrying, will you?

BLOUSEY I didn't count on this many people.

BUGSY Oh this bunch are all conjurors and magicians by the look of it. You've got no competition, believe me.

BLOUSEY How do I look?

BUGSY You look great.

BLOUSEY I look a wreck.

A **Ventriloquist** *comes on, complete with* **Dummy.**

DUMMY (*badly*) Hello everybody.

VENTRILOQUIST Well how are you, Clarence?

DUMMY Don't ask. I suppose you're wondering why I'm here.

OSCAR DE VELT You bet. Next!

The **Ventriloquist** *begins to leave. The* **Dummy** *has taken it worse than its owner. It jabbers away as they leave the stage.*

DUMMY What does he mean 'next'? Doesn't he like us? Does he know who we are? I'll punch the sucker on the nose . . .

The owner and the **Dummy** *scuffle. The* **Dummy** *seems to win.*

There follow a number of amusing acts in rapid succession. A harp player wheels on her harp but before she even gets to play we hear 'next'. There are high-kicking dancers who fall over etc. Each gets **Oscar**'s *thumbs-down 'next'. Finally it's* **Blousey**'s *turn; she moves centre stage, (or almost).*

BLOUSEY   Blousey Brown. Singer.

OSCAR DE VELT   The light, honey.

BLOUSEY   (*nervously*)   Er, sorry Mr De Velt, I didn't catch that.

OSCAR DE VELT   The light, honey. Move into the light. So we can see you. This musical ain't set in a mine shaft. Name?

BLOUSEY   Blousey Brown. Singer.

As **Blousey** *opens her mouth to sing,* **Lena Marrelli** *storms down the centre aisle.*

LENA   Oscar, Oscar . . . I'm back! I'll give you one more chance, else I'm out for good. You hear me, Oscar. Out! Out! Out!

Oscar has welcomed her and joined her as she walks on stage. **Lena** *takes over the spotlight from* **Blousey**, *cattily dismissing her.*

LENA   O.K. honey. Beat it back to Iowa, this show has got its star back. Lena's come home. Hit it, Joe!

The **Pianist** *begins.* **Lena** *belts out a horrid show business song.*

Lena *sings the first verse of her song and the spot follows her off as she carries on singing in the wings. Light on the line of auditioners who are rather dejected. They disperse in different directions.* **Bugsy** *joins* **Blousey** *who sits on the edge of the stage.*

BUGSY   Cheer up, there's a million other jobs.

BLOUSEY   Sure, on the street corner with a hat to catch the dimes in.

She kicks at a stack of cardboard boxes full of costumes.

BUGSY   It's only a matter of time. Look, cool it will you?

BLOUSEY   I've been walking the streets of New York for six months now and the only fancy steps I've done so far are avoiding the man who collects the rent.

BUGSY So it takes time to be a movie star! We could come back tomorrow.

BLOUSEY Come back tomorrow! Come back tomorrow. That's all I ever hear. I spent my whole life coming back tomorrow.

Blousey kicks the boxes of costumes once more. They topple into the orchestra.

BUGSY Knock it off will you Blousey! Cool down!

BLOUSEY I will not cool down! I will not!

Blousey has sat down on a box. She has her head in her hand. Sobbing. Bugsy consoles her, a hand on her shoulder. He loans her his handkerchief.

BUGSY Don't worry, there's always Fat Sam's place.

BLOUSEY He won't see me.

BUGSY I'll talk to him.

BLOUSEY You know him?

BUGSY Know him? We're like that (*He crosses his fingers*)

BLOUSEY Real good friends?

BUGSY No, not exactly. It's just that when I talk to him I cross my fingers that he won't hit me.

*Light up on **Radio Announcer**, left of stage. The red 'ON AIR' sign behind him. Urgently, as ever, he reads the news from the sheet of paper he holds in front of him.*

RADIO ANNOUNCER We interrupt our commentary on tonight's exciting Red-Sox ball-game to bring you a further bulletin on developments in the latest outbreak of hoodlum gang warefare. Police now officially state that the new weapon, of devious foreign manufacture, known as 'The Splurge Gun', is being widely used by the mobster gangs. We interrupt our interruption to go straight over to our reporter, Seymour Scoop, who is on the spot at the latest splurging.

Curtain up. Light on centre stage. Upturned restaurant tables. We see

gang of reporters hustling **O'Dreary,** *a detective, of Irish lineage.*
Seymour Scoop, *ace reporter, asks the questions, microphone in
hand. The wire of the microphone is attached to a* **Sound Man,** *who
has earphones. The cord is very short and* **Seymour Scoop** *very
persistent, so that the* **Soundman** *gets dragged around the stage by
his earphones.*

SEYMOUR SCOOP   Have you located the splurge gun yet,
   Lieutenant?

O'DREARY   I'm afraid I can't answer that.

SEYMOUR SCOOP   You're not at liberty to say?

O'DREARY   No, I don't know the answer.

SEYMOUR SCOOP   Have you located the source yet,
   Lieutenant?

O'DREARY   Sure I had it on my hamburger for lunch.

SEYMOUR SCOOP   No, the source of the guns.

O'DREARY   Oh. Yeah, er I mean, no. I mean I'm not at
   liberty to say. You'll have to ask Captain Smolsky that
   question. . . .

O'Dreary's *boss* **Captain Smolsky** *has entered.*

SMOLSKY   O.K. O'Dreary, break this crowd up. Let's go
   guys. Split. This is police business and police business we .
   gotta do.

SEYMOUR SCOOP   Er, Seymour Scoop, RTZ Radio, Captain
   Smolsky. Can you tell us if you have located the splurge
   guns yet?

SMOLSKY   No comment.

SEYMOUR SCOOP   Have you located the source?

SMOLSKY   No comment.

SEYMOUR SCOOP   Captain Smolsky, is it true the guns are
   being used by only one gang?

SMOLSKY   No comment.

O'DREARY   I fixed you a pastrami on rye sandwich, Chief.

SMOLSKY   No comment. O.K. get out of here.

The **Policemen** *push the* **Press Men** *off the stage.* **Smolsky** *returns
to centre stage where* **O'Dreary** *has brought on the* **Violinist.** *The*
Violinist *is a recent immigrant of Eastern European descent. His*

accent is as thick as his moustache. **Smolsky** *sits astride a bentwood chair and tips back his hat.*

SMOLSKY Now, we know there were five guys here. What else did you see?

VIOLINIST Nuttink. I see nuttink.

SMOLSKY You must have seen sometink!

VIOLINIST Nuttink. Honestly Mr Cop. I see nuttink. I came on the boat just this year. I got papers. I O.K. I see nuttink. I just play music. I mind own business. I no need cement overcoat.

O'Dreary *brushes away on the floor with his Precinct Finger-Print Kit. He blows baby powder over the clue.*

O'DREARY Captain, I found something.

SMOLSKY What is it O'Dreary?

O'DREARY A brush, Captain?

SMOLSKY No, what have you found?

O'DREARY A gun, Captain?

SMOLSKY What kind of gun?

O'DREARY A *big* gun, Captain?

Smolsky *bashes him with his hat.*

SMOLSKY Knucklehead. I send you on a six month finger print course and all you can tell me is it's a big gun! You noodle brained Irish stew-pot. (**Smolsky** *bashes him with his hat all the way to the wings.)*

We hear the 'BUGSY MALONE' song. **Bugsy** *comes on stage. One spot. He resumes his role as the narrator.*

BUGSY As you've probably gathered, Smolsky and O'Dreary have about as much chance of solving this case as I have of being President of the United States. Apart from the subway home the only thing Smolsky ever caught was Asian Flu . . . . Meanwhile back in our story, Fat Sam is definitely getting a little nervous – I mean if you had a gang of dumb bums like this to rely on you'd be nervous.

Fat Sam's Gang *enter from stage left. Lights up as they sing and dance their song. They are not the greatest dancers in the world.*

19

HOODS   *Bad Guys' Song*

We could have been anything that we wanted to be
But don't it make your heart glad
That we decided, a fact we take pride in
To become the best at being bad
We could have been anything that we wanted to be
With all the talent we had
No doubt about it, we fight and we tout it
We're the very best at being bad guys
We're rotten to the core
My congratulations, no-one likes you any more
Bad guys, we're the very worst
Each of us contemptible, we're criticised and cursed

We made the big time, malicious and mad
We're the very best at being bad
We could have been anything that we wanted to be
We took the easy way out
With little training we mastered complaining
Manners seemed unnecessary, we're so rude it's almost
    scary

We could have been anything that we wanted to be
With all the talent we had
With little practice, we made every black list
We're the very best at being bad
Hey, look at me, I'm dancing
We're the very best at being bad
We're the very best at being bad

Fat Sam *comes down from his office.*

FAT SAM   What the heck is going on here, you dummies?
    Can I believe my eyes? You bunch of peanut brains, you
    hear me? Get up here, pronto. Snap it up. Get your legs
    movin' in this direction!

The **Gang** *go up into* **Fat Sam***'s office.* **Snake Eyes** *throws his dice on
the table.* **Knuckles** *cracks his knuckles.*

Quit throwin' the dice, Snake Eyes.

SNAKE EYES   Sorry, Boss.

FAT SAM   And quit crackin' the knuckles, Knuckles.

KNUCKLES   Sorry, Boss.

FAT SAM   I swear I'm surrounded by a bunch of nervous

wrecks. (*Twitch*) Right. Let's start at the beginning. We're being outsmarted by that lounge lizard, right?

GANG   Right, Boss.

FAT SAM   And we're gonna get right back on top. Right?

GANG   Right back on top, Boss.

FAT SAM   We're gonna kick that drugstore cowboy right into line.

GANG   You bet, Boss.

FAT SAM (*humble*)   Sure. We've been a little slow off the mark, but when it comes to the crunch, dumb bums we ain't.

GANG   No – dumb bums we ain't.

Unconvincing. They look and sound remarkably like dumb bums to the audience.

FAT SAM   Now, I'm gonna tell you knuckleheads where we're going wrong. Louis. Stand against the wall.

LOUIS   Who me, Boss?

FAT SAM   Are you Shake Down Louis?

LOUIS   Sure I am, Boss.

FAT SAM   The same Shake Down Louis who used to be Harvey Spleendecker before's I gave you the name Shake Down Louis?

LOUIS   Yeah, that's me, Boss.

FAT SAM (*shouting*)   Then stand against the wall, porridge brain. Ritzy, hand me a pie.

Ritzy *hands him a mean-looking custard pie.*

LOUIS   A pie, Boss? What I do wrong? Talk to me boss. Tell me what I did wrong!

FAT SAM   You didn't do nothin' Louis. Nothin'. (*He throws the pie, but Louis ducks. The pie splatters the wall.*) See what I mean? Missed. O.K. Louis you can sit down now. See, even a dumb mug like Louis is too quick for us. That's the root of our trouble. We're behind the times.

KNUCKLES   I don't get it, Boss.

FAT SAM   Knuckles, we're never gonna get on top with this kind of hardware. It's old-fashioned. Obsolete. Defunct. In short . . . we gotta get ourselves that gun.

Light goes down on office. A light goes up left of stage. A shady looking character looks furtively over his shoulders. (Suitable dramatic music.) He is dressed in Chinese laundry clothes. He tip-toes to the phone box at the side of the stage.

SHADY Hello Sam.

Light up just on **Fat Sam.**

FAT SAM Yeah, start gabbin'.

SHADY I located the guns.

FAT SAM Spill, Shady. Spill.

SHADY You know the Hung Fu Shin laundry?

FAT SAM On East 14th Street?

SHADY That's it. 2nd Floor. Behind the laundry.

FAT SAM Thanks, Shady. I'll see you're O.K. Good boy. Dis is good news. I'll be sending my boys.

Lights down on **Fat Sam.** **Shady** *walks centre stage where he meets* **Dandy Dan** *who pays out crisp dollar bills from his crocodile skin wallet.*

DANDY DAN Good work, Shady. You earned your money.

SHADY Thanks, Dandy Dan.

DANDY DAN Sam's boys are in for quite a party. Now get out of here.

Shoulders *has walked on out of* **Shady's** *sight. He holds a pie at head height behind* **Shady.** **Shady** *turns and walks straight into it. Stiffens. Collapses.* **Dandy Dan** *retrieves his money and returns it to his wallet.*

Shoulders, if there's one thing I can't abide, its a two-timing canary.

Lights go down. There is a loud noise from the rear of the auditorium as **Louis, Ritzy** *and* **Snake Eyes** *burst in. Each carries a pie. Lights have gone up on stage revealing a number of* **Chinese Laundry Workers** *who scrub away with washboards in tin baths. Behind them are four large laundry baskets. They talk in Chinese (Well, sort of Chinese.)*

A sign says 'HUNG FU SHIN LAUNDRY'. the **Gang** *climb onto the stage. The* **Chinese Laundry Workers** *panic, running in all* *directions and jabbering away in Chinese. The* **Gang** *faces the audience, edging backwards towards the baskets. Suddenly, the basket lids are thrown open and out spring members of* **Dan's Gang**.

DAN'S GANG   Freeze!

The unfortunate **Louis, Ritzy** *and* **Snake Eyes** *are well and truly splurged.*

Dandy Dan *walks on with* **Louella**. *The* **Undertakers** *remove the stiffened bodies of* **Sam's Gang**. *The* **Violinist**, *as always, accompanies them, physically and musically, with suitable melancholic music.*

LOUELLA   Yuk, what a mess.

DANDY DAN   Just a day's work, my rose, just a day's work — like running a railway or shoeing a horse.

LOUELLA   Sam ain't gonna like this, honey.

DANDY DAN   He ain't gonna do nothin' about it, my rose. Without his gang he's like a tortoise without its shell. Soon he'll be throwin' in the towel.

Dandy Dan *and* **Louella** *bite into their apples as they walk off stage.*

Light up on **Sam's** *office.* **Knuckles** *sits on the edge of the desk as* **Sam** *takes the phone call. Bad news.*

FAT SAM   . . . What . . . ! I don't believe it! . . . The whole gang? Everybody? Louis, Snake Eyes and Ritzy? I don't believe it. I just don't believe it!

He slowly puts the receiver down.

FAT SAM   The whole gang's gone, Knuckles, splurged. That leaves just you and me. Just you and me, Knuckles! We're on our own.

KNUCKLES   What we gonna do, Boss?

Knuckles *cracks his knuckles nervously.*

FAT SAM   Don't do that, Knuckles. How many more times have I got to tell you! We do nothing. We act like nothing's happened. Carry on as normal. 'Tutto casa sono buono.'

KNUCKLES   What's that mean, Boss?

FAT SAM   You don't speak Italian?

KNUCKLES No, boss.

FAT SAM (*incredulous*) You call yourself a hoodlum and you don't even speak Italian . . . ?

KNUCKLES No boss, I'm Jewish.

FAT SAM We play it cool. We relax. Like everything's normal.

*There is a knock on the door (***Blousey***). ***Sam*** nearly jumps out of his skin as he leaps behind his desk for protection. ***Knuckles*** joins him. ***Sam*** and ***Knuckles*** would win no awards for bravery. There is another knock.*

Go see who it is, Knuckles. Act normal.

Knuckles *gets up and gingerly opens the door. It's* ***Blousey***.

KNUCKLES It's the broad about the audition, Boss. He's busy lady. Come back tomorrow.

He closes the door. ***Fat Sam*** *leaps up and opens the door. He calls out to* ***Blousey***.

FAT SAM No, wait honey! Wait. (*He turns to* ***Knuckles***) We act like normal, right? So acting normal means acting normal. (*Out of door*) We'll be right there, honey. Make yourself comfortable. We'll be a couple of minutes. Go powder your nose or somethin'. (*Closes door*) See, just like normal. That way they won't know we're scared to death . . . er, I don't mean scared I mean, er . . . concerned. We buy ourselves a little time. Thinking time, right Knuckles? Come over here, I'm gonna send for someone to help us out of our little predicament. No ten cent dummy, you hear. A specialist.

He takes a photo from his drawer.

KNUCKLES (*puzzled*) A doctor, Boss?

FAT SAM Not a doctor, you bilberry. A hoodlum.

KNUCKLES I thought we was hoodlums, Boss.

FAT SAM Not a dumb bum, Knuckles. This guy's the real McCoy.

KNUCKLES Looney Bergonzi?

FAT SAM The very same. Off his trolley, mad-as-a-hatter Bergonzi, the best man in Chicago. Right. Here's what we do. (*He snatches back the photo*) We arrange a meeting with Dandy Dan. (*He picks up the telephone and dials as he speaks*) Bergonzi will be in the back of the car – next to me. Knuckles you drive.

KNUCKLES Right. (*Pause*) But I don't drive, Boss.

FAT SAM You don't drive? You motzah head. (*Into telephone*) Oh hello! Is that Dandy Dan's residence? Could I speak to himself please. This is Sam Stacetto. Don't worry what it's about fellah, he'll know me. (*He puts his hand over the receiver as he talks to* **Knuckles**) You don't drive? Then we gotta get ourselves a driver.

There is a light up on **Dan**, *extreme left of stage. He answers the phone from his armchair. He is resplendent in his silk dressing gown and cravat.* **Louella** *sits knitting. The* **Cellist** *stands behind with a lamp shade on his/her head. He/she plays softly.*

DANDY DAN Hello. Hi Sam. What can I do for you?

FAT SAM I want to meet you Dan, to do a little talking.

DANDY DAN Where?

FAT SAM East Chester Park. Fiveways. At Lexburg and Denver. You hearing me?

DANDY DAN Yeah, I'm hearing you, Sam. But you come alone. No hoods, mind.

FAT SAM No hoods, Dan. You have my word. (*He puts hand over receiver*) What's he talking about? Don't bring your hoods – he's wiped out all my hoods. (*Back to phone*) Just you and me and our drivers.

DANDY DAN Agreed.

They both put down the phones together.

Got him, the knucklehead.

FAT SAM Got him, the salami.

Lights out on both. Lights up on speakeasy.
Fizzy *is playing the piano. Not very well.* **Bugsy** *enters. He carries a bunch of flowers.*

BUGSY Hi Fizzy.

FIZZY   Hi Bugsy.

BUGSY   How we doin'? Still practising?

FIZZY   Still practising.

BUGSY   Have you seen Blousey? I thought she was here for her audition.

FIZZY   Oh, she was here, but she went to get some air. She got tired of waiting. She left her bag so I guess she's coming back.

BUGSY   Thanks Fizzy.

Tallulah *has entered and leans on the rail at the edge of the stairs to* **Sam's** *office.*

TALLULAH   Suddenly everyone wants to be in show business.

BUGSY   Oh, hi Tallulah.

Tallulah *is joined by* **Loretta, Dotty** *and* **Tillie.**

TALLULAH   He's busy Bugsy. Why don't you have a drink while you're waiting?

BUGSY   Why not? I'll have a special on the rocks.

GIRLS   Hi Bugsy.

BUGSY   Hi Loretta . . . Dotty . . . Tillie.

TALLULAH   O.K. girls, go feed the ducks.

GIRLS   Oh Tallulah!

TALLULAH   I said beat it.

They leave the way they came. **Tallulah** *and* **Bugsy** *sit down at a table. A* **Waiter** *brings on two bright green 'specials' on a tray. He leaves.* **Fizzy** *is still tinkering with the piano.*

TALLULAH   Long time no see Bugsy.

BUGSY   Well you know how it is.

TALLULAH   You used to come and see me every night.

BUGSY   I've been busy.

TALLULAH   Doing what?

BUGSY   Oh this and that.

Tallulah *is irritated by* **Fizzy** *playing in the background.*

TALLULAH Fizzy! Will you quit the ivories and hit the shoe leather?

FIZZY Yes Ma'am.

Fizzy exits.

TALLULAH You're aces, you know that Bugsy? I've always found you kind of special.

BUGSY Careful Tallulah, you're racing my motor.

She edges closer. Very seductive.

TALLULAH Come on Bugsy, give a girl a break.

BUGSY You sure you got the right guy?

TALLULAH Oh, you're not like all those other saps.

BUGSY No?

TALLULAH You've got lovely brown eyes.

BUGSY They'll be lovely black eyes if Fat Sam catches us.

TALLULAH Come on sugar, how about smearin' my lipstick?

She pouts her lips.

BUGSY Tallulah, I'm warning, you . . . if you come any closer I'll call my lawyer.

TALLULAH So call him.

She pulls him to her and plants a smacker right on his forehead. **Blousey** *enters, with* **Razamataz**, *who is looking at her music and* **Knuckles**, *who shouts up the stairs.* **Blousey** *scowls at* **Bugsy.**

KNUCKLES Ready Boss. The broad's ready for her audition.

BUGSY Oh, hi Blousey, I was looking for you.

BLOUSEY Hush your mouth, jerk.

Fat Sam *comes down the stairs.*

FAT SAM O.K. honey, I'm all ears.

They sit astride chairs on the side of stage while **Blousey** *sits centre stage and sings to the audience.*

I'm Feeling Fine

I'm feeling fine
Filled with emotions
Stronger than wine
They give me the notion
That this strange new feeling
Is something that you're feeling too
Matter of fact, I'm forced to admit it
Caught in the act, and maybe we've hit it
Is this strange new feeling
Something that you're feeling too?

Fat Sam *listens for a while and then abruptly brings the audition to an end by clapping his hands.*

FAT SAM   O.K. honey, that's enough. Very nice. Very nice. A little too contemporary for my taste, but all the same, very nice. You're hired.

He snaps his fingers and his entourage follow him off stage. **Bugsy** *goes up to* **Blousey** *who is collecting her music.*

BUGSY   Great Blousey. That was really swell. I told you you'd make it. That was terrific, really terrific.

Blousey *is not listening. She storms off.*

Blousey! What's the matter with you? Look I can explain all that Tallulah smoochin'. . . .

Blousey *exits as* **Fat Sam** *appears from his office.*

FAT SAM   Bugsy, how'd you like to earn yourself some green stuff?

BUGSY   As long as you're not talking about cabbages. What's the catch?

FAT SAM   No catch, this is a job drivin'. Straight forward drivin'.

BUGSY   Knowing you Sam, it'll be ducking and driving. What's the pay?

FAT SAM   Two hundred.

BUGSY   Cents?

FAT SAM   No, dollars.

BUGSY   Dollars! Sounds like dangerous driving.

FAT SAM   Nah, sure it might get a little hot, but you don't get two hundred dollars for drivin' a milk truck Bugsy.

BUGSY   O.K., you got yourself a driver.

FAT SAM   Good boy. Good boy. Knuckles! Get me a drink. Things are shapin' up real fine, and I'm getting real thirsty . . . blood thirsty!

Bugsy Malone has walked up to the dressing room door. He knocks. **Bangles** *opens the door.*

BUGSY   Hi Bangles. Is Blousey there?

BANGLES   She won't see you Bugsy. She's mad. She was holding a torch for you higher than the Statue of Liberty.

BUGSY   Look, just tell her I'm sick, will you?

BANGLES   You're sick?

BUGSY   Yeah, sick of waiting here.

BANGLES   I'll see what I can do. But don't count on it.

Bugsy straightens his tie and pats the flowers. **Blousey** *appears at the door.*

BLOUSEY   Beat it wisie.

BUGSY   Give me a break Blousey. I've bought you some flowers.

She takes them.

BLOUSEY   I'll see Tallulah gets them.

BUGSY   Quit being so smart, O.K.? They're for you.

BLOUSEY   Look, I've got to go.

BUGSY   I'll see you later.

BLOUSEY   Yeah, like ten years later.

BUGSY   I've got a job.

BLOUSEY   You don't get paid for standing in breadlines buster.

BUGSY   A legit job. We'll have enough money for two tickets to the coast and Hollywood . . . Who knows, they're always looking for new stars . . .

BLOUSEY (*she interrupts*) Oh sure. I'll believe it when I see it.

FIZZY Two minutes everybody.

BLOUSEY I really have to go. Bye.

BUGSY Look Blousey, trust me.

BLOUSEY (*unconvinced*) Sure.

Blousey closes the door. **Bugsy** *walks to the front of the stage.*

BUGSY (*to audience*) I know, I know, never trust anyone who says trust me. But I was on the level, honest I was. I wanted to buy her the tickets but first I had to earn the two hundred bucks, driving Sam and Looney. Looney Bergonzi. (*Shakes head*) Boy, when they said he was off his trolley, they weren't kidding.

As he speaks various cut-out trees are placed on stage. **Bugsy** *crouches down behind a cut-out branch.* **Fat Sam** *walks on.*

FAT SAM Quick Bugsy, here he comes. Is he alone?

BUGSY MALONE Yep. Looks like just Dan and the driver.

FAT SAM Good. Looney get ready. Looney. Looney.

Looney Bergonzi *comes on. He is definitely well named. A crazed hood, carrying two enormous green-topped custard pies.*

Keep out of sight. Keep your head down. Wait 'til I give you the O.K. Right?

Looney *seems to be somewhere else.* **Fat Sam** *pats* **Looney**'s *cheeks.* **Looney** *seems to come round.* **Dandy Dan** *walks on centre stage.* **Sam** *brushes himself down and walks centre stage to meet* **Dan**.

DANDY DAN What can I do for you, Sam?

FAT SAM How about a small dose of straight talk, Dan?

DANDY DAN Suits me.

FAT SAM You've been taking liberties Dan.

DANDY DAN I've been taking what's mine.

FAT SAM Trouble is, it belongs to me.

DANDY DAN Too bad. Possession is nine tenths of the law, Sam.

FAT SAM Now hang on, Dan! I'm sure we can talk things over sensibly. We've been in this game a long time, you's and me. After all, I'm a businessman!

DANDY DAN You're a dime a dozen gangster, Sam.

FAT SAM Now you button your lip, mister. I don't like your mouth. I have to have some respect.

DANDY DAN You'd slit your own throat for two bits plus tax.

FAT SAM You keep your wise cracks behind your teeth, mister.

DANDY DAN Keep talking.

FAT SAM I have my position to think of.

DANDY DAN Right now, your position ain't worth a plug nickel.

FAT SAM You dirty rat, Dan. (*James Cagney-ish*)

DANDY DAN (*smiling*) You've been watching too many movies Sam.

FAT SAM O.K. Looney, let him have it!

*Looney leaps from behind a tree. His green pies seem to be at the ready, but there doesn't seem to be much intelligence flickering behind his crazy, staring eyes. **Bugsy** still crouches behind the cut-out bush.*

DANDY DAN Yonkers! Charlie! Quick, it's a double-cross!

*Dan's Gang appear from behind the other cut-out trees. They have their splurge guns at the ready. They approach **Looney** and splurge him considerably before he can react. He collapses. Rigid. **Bugsy** takes the initiative. He grabs the petrified **Sam**.*

BUGSY Come on Mr Stacetto, let's get out of here!

*The lights go out. The spots sweep the stage. There is much shouting and activity as everyone runs back and forth across the stage. Confusion. **Bugsy** guides **Sam** off the stage and they do a complete circle of the auditorium. When they arrive back on stage, **Dan** and his gang are gone.*

FAT SAM (*out of breath*) You did great, Bugsy. Great. Here's your two hundred dollars, and a hundred extra for your quick thinking.

BUGSY Gee, thanks Mr Stacetto.

FAT SAM   Treat yourself to a new suit. Get rid of that laundry sack you're wearing. Here's the name of my tailor. (*He hands him a card*)

BUGSY   Thanks Mr Stacetto.

FAT SAM   Think nothing of it. My pleasure. Right now, let's get out of here.

They exit. Light up on **Blousey** *to one side of the stage.*

BLOUSEY (*slower than normal*)

Hot headed Bugsy makes his mind up
Don't mess with Bugsy, or you'll wind up
Wishing you'd let well enough alone.
He's a man, a mountain, a rolling stone.
And will he leave you sad and lonely
Crying – I couldn't stay – But it's known
That everybody loves that man – Bugsy Malone.

Lights down.
Black.

END OF ACT ONE

ACT TWO

The stage is set as the girls' dressing room. There are racks of clothes etc. **Tillie**, **Loretta** *etc. and the rest of the chorus join in as* **Tallulah** *does her number.*

My Name is Tallulah

My name is Tallulah
My first rule of thumb
I don't say where I'm going
Or where I'm coming from
I try to leave a little reputation behind me
So if you really need to
You'll know how to find me

My name is Tallulah
I live till I die
I'll take what you give me
And I won't ask why
I've made a lot of friends
In some exotic places
I don't remember names
But I remember faces

*Lonely, you don't have to be lonely
Come and see Tallulah
We can chase your troubles away
If you're lonely
You don't have to be lonely
When they talk about Tallulah
You know what they say
No-one south of heaven's gonna treat you finer
Tallulah had her training
In North Carolina

My name is Tallulah
And soon I'll be gone
An open invitation
Is the road I'll travel on
I'll never say goodbye
Because the words upset me

You may forgive my going
But you won't forget me

*Repeat

At the end of the number we hear a phone ring. **Tallulah** answers it.

TALLULAH   Yeah sure, I'll get her. Blousey! It's for you.

Blousey goes to the phone.

(sarcastically)   Give him my love.

The lights come up on **Bugsy** in the phone booth at the side of the stage.

BLOUSEY   Hello.

BUGSY   Hey Blousey, it's Bugsy.

BLOUSEY   Where are you?

BUGSY   Oh around. Listen. I can't talk to you now, but I've just made two hundred bucks.

BLOUSEY   You mean you printed it yourself?

BUGSY   No I earned it, swear to God. (Crosses himself)

BLOUSEY   Doing what?

BUGSY   Oh this and that.

BLOUSEY   Who for?

BUGSY   Fat Sam.

BLOUSEY   Fat Sam gave you 200 dollars?

BUGSY   And the loan of his sedan for the afternoon.

BLOUSEY   I don't believe you. You're putting me on.

BUGSY   Look, if you get yourself outside the Grand Slam in ten minutes, look for the snazzy sedan with the good lookin' driver and you'll find he has a very close resemblance to yours truly . . . O.K.. . . ?

BLOUSEY   O.K. But you'd better not be putting me on, Buster.

BUGSY   Cross my heart it's on the level. So long.

The light goes down on **Bugsy** and **Blousey** puts on her hat and coat and exits during the next scene.

34

BANGLES   Date Blousey?

BLOUSEY   Sort of.

BANGLES   I'm giving up guys, they're nothin' but trouble, believe me. From now on I'm lookin' for husbands. And I ain't getting too attached. I'm gonna change 'em regular like a library book. Hey! Don't you think I look cute? What do you think of the dress Tillie?

TILLIE   I don't know, it's . . .

BANGLES   Come on Dotty, what do you think?

DOTTY   Er, well, I don't know Bangles, maybe the colour's wrong.

BANGLES   What are you talking about? Purple's my colour. I always wear purple.

LORETTA (*sarcastically*)   Yeah, it matches the veins in your legs.

DOTTY   Maybe it's the length.

BANGLES   It's the latest length. I read it in a magazine.

VELMA   Maybe it's the frills, they stick out too much.

LORETTA   They match her ears.

BANGLES (*angry*)   Do you think it'll look any better on you?

LORETTA   It'll look better on a horse.

BANGLES   You're just jealous. Can I help it if my looks are ahead of my time?

ALL   They're what?

BANGLES (*sexily*)   Full of personality . . . character . . . kinda *earthy* . . .

TALLULAH   Yeah, like a bucket of mud.

The girls all laugh as **Bangles** *storms out. Lights down. Musical reprise of 'I'M FEELING FINE'. Lights up on side of stage where* **Blousey** *is sitting on a swing.* **Bugsy** *enters with two hot dogs.*

BUGSY   Mustard with onions, Ketchup without.

BLOUSEY   Ketchup without. Do you really have 200 dollars?

BUGSY   Nope.

BLOUSEY   Oh yeah, you lied.

BUGSY   No, I've got 198 dollars and ten cents – I just bought two hot dogs.

BLOUSEY   You didn't do anything crooked, did you?

BUGSY   Of course not. I got it for driving and for helping Mr Sam out of a little predicament. Oh, I nearly forgot.

He hands a parcel to her. A big shoe-box tied with a ribbon.

BLOUSEY   What's this, a fingerbowl?

BUGSY   No, a present wisie!

BLOUSEY   For me?

BUGSY (*he looks around him*)   Well I didn't buy it for the audience . . .

BLOUSEY   Oh Bugsy, it's wonderful. Fantastic. What is it?

She looks through the wrong end of an old photo viewer.

BUGSY   A viewer, dummy. (*He turns it round the correct way*) Look, you turn the handle. All the Hollywood stars.

BLOUSEY   Oh, if only I could get to Hollywood.

BUGSY   You can.

BLOUSEY   Oh sure, I've heard that one, wise guy . . . in the front row of the Roxy on East 38th Street.

BUGSY   No, *really* get to Hollywood.

She beckons back with her thumb.

You want me to leave?

BLOUSEY   No, *push* me, dummy, and keep talking . . .

BUGSY   I've got 198 dollars and 10 cents left, right? What does that buy?

BLOUSEY   Er . . . (*Counting on her fingers*) 440 hot dogs.

BUGSY   No, two tickets, stupid.

BLOUSEY   Two tickets?

BUGSY   On the Super Chief.

BLOUSEY   Super Chief ?

BUGSY   The train, dummy! To Hollywood. Think about it.

There is silence. **Bugsy** *moves away and starts to clean his fingers with a napkin.*

BLOUSEY (*swinging and singing to herself*)
I'm feeling fine.
Filled with emotions
Stronger than wine
They give me the notion
That this strange new feeling
Is something that you're feeling too.
. . . too . . . too . . .

Two tickets?

BUGSY (*over his shoulder*)   Yeah, two tickets.

BLOUSEY (*singing quietly*)   Matter of fact, I'm forced to
admit it, I'm caught in the act, and maybe we've hit it, If
this strange new feeling is something that you're feeling
too . . . oo . . . oo . . .

BUGSY   So what's the answer?

BLOUSEY   Did you honestly think it'd be anything but yes?
Oh Bugsy . . . (*She embraces him*) Hollywood!

BUGSY   Knock it off will you?

BLOUSEY   You're putting me on!

BUGSY   It's the honest truth I tell you. (*Kisses his finger,
touches her on the nose.*) It's just that if I don't get this
sedan back soon Fat Sam will have my face looking like a
plateful of yesterday's fetucinni.

*They walk off arm in arm. Lights down. We hear dramatic sleuthing
type music.* **Smolsky** *and* **O'Dreary** *come on. They are examining the
ground with large magnifying glasses. They separate across the stage
in different directions.*

SMOLSKY   Ahaa . . . ! I think I've found something. Come
and take a look at this, O'Dreary.

O'Dreary *obediently runs to where his boss is crouched.*

O'DREARY   You've cracked it this time, Captain Smolsky.

SMOLSKY   I have? (*Surprised*) What do you see? Tell me,
what do you see, O'Dreary?

O'DREARY (*carefully looking down*)   Your foot, Captain?

Smolsky *takes off his hat and hits* **O'Dreary** *with it.*

SMOLSKY   Not my foot, knucklehead. *Under* my foot. Tyre
marks!

O'DREARY   Oh, it's a tyre mark all right, Captain.

SMOLSKY   Too right it's a tyre mark, you Irish potato head. Get some plaster. We'll take a mould.

O'Dreary runs off. **Smolsky** *looks around for more clues.*

There ought to be more marks. There sure as eggs is eggs was more than one sedan around here. Hey, what's this?

He kneels down and **O'Dreary** *promptly trips over him as he enters, pouring the white liquid over his boss.*

Aaaaaah!

O'DREARY   Gee Captain. I'm sorry sir, I didn't see you there, honestly I didn't . . .

SMOLSKY   You dumb potato face Irish jerk!

He chases him around the stage.

O'DREARY   Couldn't help it, Captain . . . Gee, I'm sorry, Captain Smolsky. It was an accident, honestly.

SMOLSKY   If I catch you, O'Dreary, I'm gonna punch that stupid Irish nose right back to Tipperary.

They run off, stage right. **Fat Sam** *and* **Knuckles** *come on.* **Knuckles** *carries a strange contraption that looks like a mad combination of machine gun and butcher's mincer.* **Sam** *carries a cardboard cut-out of* **Dandy Dan**. *He sits it up on one side of the stage as* **Knuckles** *prepares the 'gun' on the other.*

KNUCKLES   You sure this is going to work, Boss? (*Cracks his knuckles*)

FAT SAM   Of course it is. Knuckles, don't crack your knuckles, it makes me nervous.

KNUCKLES   Sorry, Boss.

FAT SAM   Of course it'll work. It looks like a splurge gun, doesn't it?

Knuckles *shakes his head.*

FAT SAM (*threatening*)   Doesn't it?

KNUCKLES   Er . . . sure Boss, kind of . . . (*He frowns*)

FAT SAM Anything Dandy Dan can do, Fat Sam can do better. Am I right or am I right?

KNUCKLES (*pondering the alternative*) You're right, Boss.

FAT SAM Right. Now, are you ready, Knuckles?

KNUCKLES Sure thing, Boss.

FAT SAM O.K. Get set . . .

KNUCKLES I'm set, Boss.

FAT SAM . . . and FIRE!

The gun explodes in a fountain of creamy splurge and clouds of smoke.
Knuckles *is covered in splurge and staggers around as* **Fat Sam** *goes to examine the cut-out of* **Dandy Dan**.

Missed! Back to the drawing board, Knuckles.

Meanwhile **Knuckles** *has staggered across the stage in a semi-stiff state and finally collapsed just out of sight behind the side of the stage.*

Knuckles . . . speak to me, Knuckles . . . Knuckles!

He runs back and punches the cut-out of **Dan**.

It's all your fault, I'll get you for this, you greasy lounge lizard . . . Knuckles. (*Crying almost*) Poor Knuckles . . . (*He rushes off left*)

Bugsy *enters right, whistling 'I'M FEELING FINE'.*

BUGSY (*to audience, as he sweeps and tidies up*) As you can see from the mess here, things are looking kind of untidy in Fat Sam's life . . . and as for Knuckles . . . well, whatever game it was he was playing, he'd sure cashed his chips in, and as for Captain Smolsky . . . well, he started out with the intention of chasing O'Dreary back to County Cork except he forgot that he'd had quick drying plaster poured all over him and very soon he was stiffer than some of those dudes he'd occasionally dragged out of the East River . . . *There is a moan from the back of the stage.* . . . anyway . . .

Further moaning sound. **Bugsy** *walks to the back of the stage. There are a number of garbage cans and boxes of assorted rubbish.* **Bugsy** *approaches carefully. More moans.*

Hello, is anybody there? Hello . . .

Moan.

. . . are you hurt?

Suddenly he is jumped on by the man he is trying to help and four other down-and-outs who appear from behind the garbage cans. They start to beat him up. Suddenly **Leroy** *enters from stage right. He rushes to* **Bugsy**'s *rescue, punching out the unfortunate down-and-outs in all directions. His punching power is awesome. His work done, he picks up* **Bugsy** *from the garbage cans.*

LEROY They take your money, mister?

BUGSY (*tapping his pockets*) Yeah, 200 dollars less 90 cents. It was sure nice of you to help me like that.

LEROY Oh, it was nothing.

BUGSY You must be a boxer, right?

LEROY Nope!

BUGSY You're not? But that's the best punching I've ever seen.

LEROY Oh, it was nothing.

BUGSY You ever been coached?

LEROY Nope.

BUGSY You ever thought of taking it up, I mean professionally?

LEROY Nope.

BUGSY Why not? You could be a champion.

LEROY Never thought about it.

BUGSY You haven't?

LEROY Never had the chance.

BUGSY I know someone who could help you. You know Cagey Joe?

LEROY Nope.

BUGSY You know Sluggers' Gym?

LEROY Nope.

BUGSY You don't know much, do you?

LEROY (*big warm smile*) Nope.

40

BUGSY Put it there, Leroy, you've got yourself a manager.

As they exit right, the lights go up and the stage is filled with **Boxers** *who are busy skipping, punching bags, sparring, exercising.*
Bugsy *and* **Leroy** *enter from down the stairs.*

BUGSY Hi, Cagey Joe!

CAGEY JOE Hi, Bugsy. How you been, man?

BUGSY Swell, Cagey Joe, real swell. And you?

CAGEY JOE For me, yeah. But this bunch of punch bags, the pits.

BUGSY Cagey Joe, I want you to meet the next heavyweight champion. Leroy, meet Cagey Joe. Cagey Joe, meet Leroy Smith.

CAGEY JOE (*circling* **Leroy** *and nervously removing his hat*) Ever been in the ring before, boy?

LEROY Nope.

CAGEY JOE So you wanna be a fighter, huh?

LEROY Er, nope.

BUGSY Sure he does. Look at those mits. Did you ever see such shillelaghs? Hit it Leroy.

Leroy *punches* **Bugsy**'s *out-stretched hand, very hard.* **Bugsy** *winces.* **Cagey** *is impressed.*

CAGEY JOE What's your name again, kid?

LEROY Leroy Smith.

BUGSY With you showing him the ropes, Cagey Joe, he could be champion in no time.

CAGEY JOE O.K. I'll give him a try. But I'll tell you now, he'll be no good unless he's got 'it'.

LEROY 'It'? What's 'it'?

He stares at his hands as if 'it' is some kind of disease.

BUGSY 'It' is the difference between being a no-hoper slugger and being a champion.

CAGEY JOE It's what makes a fighter special. If you haven't got 'it', you just haven't got it.

So You Wanna Be a Boxer

So you wanna be a boxer
In the golden ring
Can you punch like a south-bound freight train?
Tell me just one thing
Can you move in a whirl
Like a humming-bird's wing
If you need to? (That's fast)
Can you bob, can you weave
Can you fake and deceive
When you need to?
Well you might as well quit
If you haven't got it
So you wanna be a boxer
Can you pass the test?
I can tell if you've got it in you
I've trained the best
When you work and you sweat and you bet
That you train to a buzz-saw
Then you near lose your mind when you find that
Your boy has a glass jaw
So you might as well quit
If you haven't got it
Put him in the ring Joe
Look at what you found
We can use the fun Joe
Pushing him around
We'll show him the ropes
And destroy his hopes
Put him in the ring Joe
Give the guy a chance
Let him feel the sting Joe
We can make him dance
We'll pulp him to bits
Then he'll call it quits
For sure Joe
So you want to be a boxer
Want to be the champ
There's a golden boy inside you
Not a punched-out tramp
If you listen and you learn
There's an honour you can earn and defend here
When you do see the crown
You're a king, not a clown

A contender
But you might as well quit
If you haven't got it
Put him in the ring Joe
Something new to punch
Let me have a swing Joe
Then we'll go to lunch
We'll make it quite swift
Then he'll get the drift
Put him in the ring Joe
Chicken a la carte
Let me have a wing Joe
Tearing him apart
That chicken will crow
Oh, let me have him Joe

During the song **Leroy** *has his jacket and shirt removed and gloves put on his hands. The other* **Boxers** *form the ring on three sides. A bell sounds at the end of the song and* **Leroy** *and his (large) opponent encircle one another, gloves held high.* **Leroy** *only throws one massive punch, but it is enough to floor his larger, burly opponent.*

ALL Cheers.

CAGEY JOE He's got it.

ALL He's got it. He's got it. He's got it.

Leroy *is centre stage front, taking the congratulatory back slaps. He stares at his lethal fists. He can't quite believe it either.*

LEROY I've got it!

Lights down. Lights up on **Fat Sam**'s *office.*

Sam *is sitting at his desk. Worried.* **Tallulah** *sits on the edge of the desk painting her nails. The phone rings.* **Sam** *grabs it.*

FAT SAM Hello . . . what? . . . They got to the still . . . Not the sarsaparilla racket?

A black boy tied up from head to toe is propped up in the telephone booth as he speaks. His name is **Pickett**.

PICKETT It's gone, Boss. They got to the still. They had axes and chopped away at the barrels – it's all gone – drained away. Every last drop.

FAT SAM Oh no. Pickett, get round here right away.

PICKETT I can't, Boss. I'm all tied up.

FAT SAM I don't care how busy you are, get round here right away.

The lights dim on the unfortunate **Pickett**.

The phone rings again.

FAT SAM No, not the grocery racket? No. O.K. O.K. No, I'm sure you did all you could. Go home and get washed up.

He puts the phone down very slowly. He strokes the edge of his cocktail glass.

FAT SAM That's the whole empire gone, Tallulah. You hear me? Everything. And they'll be coming here next. There's only one thing for it. You'll have to get him to help me.

TALLULAH (*ultra cool*) Who? The Lone Ranger?

FAT SAM No, you dumb Dora. Bugsy Malone. Call him.

Tallulah *picks up the phone and dials.*

I'm in trouble, real trouble, and all I got for company is a female comedian.

TALLULAH No answer.

FAT SAM I want you to go ask him for help. Personally. (*Pronounced 'Poysonally'*)

TALLULAH Poysonally?

FAT SAM (*adamantly*) Poysanally.

TALLULAH Poysanally. So long lover boy.

Tallulah *blows him a kiss, and walks down the steps as the lights dim on* **Sam**'s *office.*

Lights up on centre. **Bugsy** *is pacing up and down waiting for* **Blousey**. *His suitcase at the ready.*

TALLULAH Hi, Bugsy.

Bugsy *turns quickly.*

BUGSY Blousey! Oh, it's you, Tallulah.

As he does so he trips over his suitcase.

TALLULAH I like my men at my feet.

BUGSY What are you doing here, Tallulah?

TALLULAH Put your flaps down, tiger, else you'll take off. I've got a message for you.

BUGSY So what's wrong with Western Union?

TALLULAH Don't flatter yourself, tiger, it's Sam who wants to see you. Not me. Come on, let's go before your suspender belt strangles you.

BUGSY I'm, waiting for someone.

TALLULAH You are?

BUGSY For Blousey, we're going to Hollywood.

TALLULAH Well, you know what they say. Don't pack anything you can't put on the train home. Sam's in trouble, Bugsy . . . and I'm sure he'll see you're O.K.

She rubs her fingers together indicating money. **Bugsy**, *who is broke, needs no more incentive.*

BUGSY I'll be right there.

They exit right of stage. Lights up reveal a couple of speakeasy tables and a small bar with bottles on it. A barman **Joe** *clears the glasses as* **Sam** *stalks nervously down the stairs from his office.* **Fizzy** *washes the floor with a mop. He whistles, as usual.*

FAT SAM Quit whistling, Fizzy, it makes me edgy.

FIZZY Sure, Boss.

FAT SAM (*to barman*) Joe.

JOE Yes, boss.

FAT SAM Fix me a double on the rocks.

JOE Sure thing, Boss.

As he pours the drink he notices the drooping flower in **Sam**'s *lapel. He can't hold back a sly snigger.*

FAT SAM So what's funny, mister? You find me amusing?

JOE Nothing, Boss . . . N . . . n . . . no I wasn't smiling at you, honest I wasn't.

FAT SAM   You find my suit comical perhaps?

JOE   Oh no, Boss. It was just your flower.

FAT SAM   Oh yeah . . . It's kind of . . . droopy ain't it.

JOE (*laughing nervously*)   Yeah, a little, Boss.

FAT SAM   In fact, *very* droopy.

JOE   Yeah Boss, very droopy.

FAT SAM   Here, hold it a minute will you? It needs a little water.

Sam passes the flower to **Joe** *who holds it while* **Sam** *picks up a jug of water. He viciously empties the contents in* **Joe**'s *face. He grabs him by the shirt and pulls him towards him.*

Now don't let me see you laughing at me again, you hear me, else I'll ram that smile right down your throat. I'm Fat Sam. Don't forget that. Number one man! Top dog! Mr Big! Always have been. Always will be.

As he walks across the wet floor he falls flat on his back.

FIZZY (*after the event*)   Careful, Boss. The floor's wet.

FAT SAM (*running after him*)   You stupid broom-pushing no-good hoofer. I'll break that mop over your head . . . ! You . . . ! You . . . !

Bugsy enters. **Fat Sam** *abruptly changes his aggressive mood, and opens his arms to* **Bugsy**.

Oh, hi Bugsy. Glad you could make it. How you been?

BUGSY   Fine Mr Stacetto. And you?

FAT SAM   Oh, a little difficulty at the moment Bugsy. Please call me Sam. Why don't you pull up a chair and sit down? Tallulah honey, fix him a drink will you?

TALLULAH   What's your pleasure, Bugsy?

BUGSY   Special on the rocks, Tallulah, please.

FAT SAM (*lowering his voice*)   Bugsy, I need your help. I'm in a jam. Dandy Dan's breathing down my neck, and any day now he'll be taking over my entire organisation.

BUGSY   But you've still got all this. (*Gestures around speakeasy*)

FAT SAM Not if Dandy Dan gets his way. I won't have a dime for a shoe-shine.

BUGSY Nothing?

FAT SAM Not a red cent.

*Tallulah has brought **Bugsy**'s drink and sits herself down. **Sam** doesn't want her there.*

TALLULAH There we go, one special on the rocks.

FAT SAM Er .. Tallulah, go fix your make up.

TALLULAH I've already fixed it.

FAT SAM Then go make yourself more beautiful than you already are.

TALLULAH But you know that's impossible.

FAT SAM (*firmly*) Tallulah . . . !

TALLULAH O.K. O.K. I'll go manicure my gloves.

She struts offstage, left.

FAT SAM Bugsy, I need help. My gang's gone. My friends don't want to know me. My business ain't worth a hill of beans. I'm a wreck. In short, Bugsy, I need *you.*

BUGSY Me Sam? Why me?

FAT SAM 'Cause you're no mug. You've got brains – up here. (*Touches temple*) Not pretzels.

BUGSY No. Rough stuff ain't my line.

FAT SAM Help me and I'll give you two hundred bucks to go with the two hundred I already gave you.

BUGSY Impossible.

FAT SAM I thought you were smart?

BUGSY Impossible, because I already lost the first two hundred.

FAT SAM You lost two hundred bucks. On a horse?

BUGSY No, I was mugged.

FAT SAM (*taking out his wallet and counting out the money*) Tut, tut. Too many dishonest people around these days Bugsy. A hoodlum ain't safe walking the streets. Here. Two hundred green ones. Plus . . . the two hundred that you lost.

BUGSY Four hundred dollars!

FAT SAM Do we have a deal? Well?

BUGSY (*fanning out the money*) We have a deal.

A phone rings. Lights up on the telephone booth, side of stage.
Blousey *is there. She has her suitcase with her.* **Tallulah** *answers the phone in the speakeasy.*

BLOUSEY Hello. Is Bugsy there, please?

TALLULAH Sure, I'll get him for you, honey. Bugsy, it's for you. It's Blousey.

BUGSY Excuse me a minute, Sam.

FAT SAM Sure thing, Bugsy. Take it in my office. Use the phone all you want. Treat this place as your own. Phone home. Phone Europe. Phone wherever you want. (*Nervous laugh*) After all, if Dandy Dan takes over this place he'll be paying the phone bill. Ha ha. (*His laugh fools no one*)

Bugsy *counts the money as he trots up the stairs to* **Sam**'s *room to take the call. Lights down on* **Sam**, *up on* **Bugsy**.

BUGSY Hello Blousey.

BLOUSEY Bugsy, is that you? What are you doing there? We said eight-thirty and you're an hour late.

BUGSY Something came up.

BLOUSEY Like what?

BUGSY Like business.

BLOUSEY Oh yeah, with Tallulah?

BUGSY Not with Tallulah, wisie.

BLOUSEY Did you get the tickets?

BUGSY Er, no. Not yet. I told you, something's come up.

BLOUSEY You promised me, Bugsy. You promised me.

BUGSY I know, but this is business, Blousey, and it can't wait. Hollywood can.

BLOUSEY An hour I've been waiting here, Bugsy, and when first you didn't show I gave you the benefit of the doubt and then I got nervous and called every pool hall dive in the phone book. They hadn't seen you but, boy, did they all know you!

Tallulah has brought **Bugsy**'s *drink from downstairs. As she puts it down on the desk she gives* **Bugsy** *a gentle peck on the side of the cheek.*

BUGSY   Get off, Tallulah.

BLOUSEY   You rat. You two timin' bog Irish meatball wop!

She slams the phone down. All lights go out except on her. She cries and walks forward with her suitcase, front of stage. She sits on her case and sings.

Ordinary Fool

Only a fool like fools before me
I always think with my heart
Only a fool, that same old story
Seems I was born for the part

*It's a lesson that I've learned
And a page I should have turned
I shouldn't cry but I do
Like an ordinary fool
When her ordinary dreams
Fall through

How many times have I mistaken
Good looks and laughs
For bad news
How many times have I mistaken
Love songs and laughs
For the blues
When a road I've walked before
Ends alone at my front door
I shouldn't cry but I do
Like an ordinary fool
When her ordinary dreams
Fall through

*Repeat twice

At the end of the song **Blousey** *picks up her bag and leaves stage left. Lights down.* **Bugsy** *enters from the audience. He calls* **Leroy**'s *name into the dark stage*

BUGSY   Leroy. Hey, Leroy, wake up. Come on. Leroy!

Leroy enters in his pyjamas. He has obviously been woken from a deep sleep. He carries a window, which he props up and peers out of, behind a curtain.

LEROY   Who is it? What do you want?

BUGSY   It's me, Leroy, Bugsy. Get dressed and come with me. We got a job.

LEROY   You got me a crack at the title already?

BUGSY   No, this is a different kind of job.

Leroy ducks backs into his window.

LEROY   I'm tired, Bugsy. Come back in the morning.

Leroy leaves the stage. **Bugsy** *perseveres.*

BUGSY   It'll be too late in the morning.

No reply.

> You'll be working for Fat Sam Stacetto. You'll be hitting Dandy Dan where it hurts . . . (*Last chance*) er . . . and there's two hundred dollars in it for you.

Leroy appears immediately on this last line. He is fully dressed, plus hat.

LEROY   I'll do it!

Leroy jumps down and joins **Bugsy**. *They exit right.*

Light up on the speakeasy. The **Girls** *sit at the tables, talking quietly. There is an air of uneasy expectancy.* **Fizzy** *sweeps and whistles his tune 'TOMORROW'.* **Blousey** *enters left with her suitcase.* **Fat Sam** *comes down the stairs of his office. He claps his hands.*

FAT SAM   Come on you guys, this place is like a morgue. Let's have a little optimism here. We're not on Poverty Row yet. How about some music?

The piano plays 'TOMORROW' and the girls join in, gently humming the melody.

> Oh, hi Blousey, I thought you was on your way to the coast.

BLOUSEY It fell through.

FAT SAM Oh, shame. Tough.

BLOUSEY Mr Stacetto, do you think I could have my job back?

FAT SAM Sure honey, go right in. The more the merrier. (*He moves off*)

The girls spot **Blousey.**

BANGLES Hi Blousey. D'you miss your train?

TILLIE Hi Blousey, what happened? Your guy let you down?

Velma *and* **Tallulah** *have come down the stairs.*

VELMA Hi Blousey, how you been?

Blousey *says nothing. She brushes past them and exits up the stairs.*

Did you ever see a broad carry a torch so high?

TALLULAH Yeah, the Statue of Liberty.

Lights down.
Spotlight on **Bugsy** *and* **Leroy**, *side of the stage, behind a couple of barrels. They look out to one side of the audience. A sign above them says 'DOCK 17'.*

BUGSY Ssh. There's a truck pulling up. Splurge guns.

LEROY (*looking around*) Where?

BUGSY On the crates, stupid. Look what it says on the side of the truck.

LEROY I can't.

BUGSY Can't you read?

LEROY (*lying*) Er . . . no, just a little shortsighted. What does it say?

BUGSY It says: 'Splurge Imports Inc. Dock 17, East River.' This must be the place where they keep the guns.

LEROY Well, let's go.

Bugsy *restrains him.*

BUGSY Hold your horses. There must be a dozen guards there.

LEROY There are?

BUGSY Two on the roof. Two on the side. Two on the front . . . It's no good just the two of us. What we gonna do, Leroy?

LEROY Go home?

BUGSY There must be a way in.

LEROY Don't be stupid, Bugsy. We'll never slug our way through that lot.

BUGSY I guess you're right. We'd need an army to get through.

LEROY (*looking around him*) No armies around here, Bugsy.

We hear the beginnings of the 'DOWN AND OUTS' song, very softly accompanied by the shuffling of their feet in unison.

DOWN AND OUTS Down. Down. Down and out. Down. Down. Down and out.

BUGSY What's that?

LEROY What? (*He looks in the barrel*)

BUGSY Listen.

The 'DOWN AND OUTS' chorus gets louder. **Bugsy** *and* **Leroy** *walk to centre stage as the lights go up on the main stage which now is filled with lines of the wretched* **Down and Outs** *who shuffle around the stage. They have bowls and spoons in their hands. There is also a* **Priest** *and some kindly lady* **Cooks** *who ladle out 'soup'. A large sign above them says: 'THE LORD WILL PROVIDE'.* **Leroy** *and* **Bugsy** *mingle among these unfortunates, trying to persuade them to join their cause.*

Down and Out

You don't have to sit around
Complaining 'bout the way your life has wound up
Think of all the time you waste
And time's a precious thing to let roll by
Sure you've hit the bottom
But remember you'll be building from the ground up
Every day's another step
That takes you even closer to the sky
So give it a try
You don't have to sit around
Depressed about the way that luck deceived you

Fortune sailed away
You missed the boat
And found that you'd been left behind
Fight and fight some more
Until you know the world is ready to receive you
Lady Luck is fickle
But a lady is allowed to change her mind
You don't have to sit around
Complaining about the way your life has wound up
So be a man
You know you can't be certain
that you'll lose until you try
You don't have to sit 'bout
Complaining about the way your life has wound up
So be a man
You know you can't be certain
that you'll lose until you try
So give it a try

At the end of the song **Bugsy** *shouts to the* **Down and Outs**.

BUGSY   Are you with me?

DOWN AND OUTS   Yeah!

BUGSY   Then let's go . . . !

They all rush and crowd to stage right. They crouch for cover as best they can. Lights come up on stage left and **Baseball Guards** *armed with baseball bats bring on crates. 'Splurge Imports Inc.' is stencilled on each one. They form a wall between them and the* **Down and Outs**. *The* **Baseball Guards** *lounge around.*

BUGSY   Right, there they are. All ready for the taking. Get Babyface.

LEROY   Get Babyface.

The message is repeated by everyone as it is passed down the line. **Babyface** *is closest to the audience, and is the last to get the message. He has no one to pass it on to.*

BABYFACE   Get Babyface. (*to audience*) Er, is there anyone called Babyface out there? What am I talking about? I am Babyface.

BUGSY   Give this to Babyface.

He passes along a baseball bat and each **Down and Out** *repeats the message as it goes down the line.*

BABYFACE   No thanks. (*Passes it back*)

BUGSY   Babyface – get out there . . .

BABYFACE   O.K. O.K. I've got to have courage. Courage. I'm the star of this play right now. (*His face lights up*) Just think. The star of (*As appropriate*) School. O.K. Courage.

He straightens his cap and tip-toes up to the **Guards**. *At the last minute he rushes and bashes a* **Guard** *over the head.*

Geronimo!!

The other **Guards** *immediately charge after him. He leaps from the stage and exits from the auditorium chased by all the* **Baseball Guards**. *Immediately they've left,* **Bugsy** *and the rest of the* **Guards** *charge across the stage and begin to open the crates.*

Smolsky and **O'Dreary**, *with six* **Policemen** *appear from down the steps and take up a position opposite them, stage right.*

Smolsky carries a megaphone.

SMOLSKY   O.K. we know you're in there.

The **Down and Outs**, **Leroy** *and* **Bugsy** *freeze.*

I'll give you ten seconds to give yourselves up. Come up without your irons and with your hands up in the air.

LEROY   What we gonna do, Bugsy?

BUGSY   I don't know, Leroy.

SMOLSKY   Right. This is your last warning. I'm gonna start counting now. One. Two. Three. Four. Five . . . er . . . Five . . . er . . .

O'DREARY   Six, Captain Smolsky. The next number is six.

Smolsky bashes **O'Dreary** *with his hat.*

SMOLSKY   I know! I know! Six . . . seven . . . eight . . .

Meanwhile a **Down and Out** *has climbed onto* **Leroy**'s *shoulders and examines the top of the stairs up stage.*

LEROY   Bugsy, look, there's a trap door here – another way out.

BUGSY O.K. Quick. Let's go.

They exit.

SMOLSKY I'm warning you guys. Don't think I'm bluffing.
We'll be coming in and you'll get what's coming to you.
Nine . . . Ten . . . O.K. O'Dreary, this is it. Ten . . .
(*Nervously*) We're going in.

O'DREARY When ever you say, Captain.

SMOLSKY Ten!

O'DREARY Ten!

SMOLSKY Ready? Now!

They all charge across the stage and find **Bugsy** *and his* **Down and
Outs** *have fled.*

They're not here, O'Dreary. Where did they go? Where did
they go?

O'DREARY Somewhere else, Captain.

Smolsky *bashes* **O'Dreary** *once more with his hat. They all charge
back across the stage and exit right.*

The lights come up at the top of the left staircase where **Dandy Dan**
*reviews his gang. They are all carrying splurge guns, and look very
confident.* **Dan** *is dapper as ever.*

DANDY DAN O.K. gang. This is the caper that's gonna take
the lid off City Hall. This is the big one.

GANG The big one.

DANDY DAN The shakedown.

GANG The shakedown.

DANDY DAN This is the pay-off.

GANG The pay-off.

DANDY DAN It's got to be good. Got to be neat. Got to be
quick.

GANG Got to be quick. Got to be neat. Got to be . . .

DANDY DAN Quit repeating everything I say. You
shouldn't have any trouble. Just Sam and a few dance-hall
girls.

The **Gang** *laugh.*

Remember when you get inside that speakeasy, keep those fingers pumping because it'll be history you'll be writing.

YONKERS Three cheers for Dandy Dan. Hip hip, hooray.

DANDY DAN Too kind, guys. Too kind. Now for Fat Sam's Grand Slam.

They exit left at the top of their platform.

The lights go up and the stage is filled with **Down and Outs,** **Dancers, Bugsy, Leroy, Tallulah, Blousey** *and* **Fat Sam.** *Everyone is moving and busily preparing for the showdown with* **Dandy Dan** *and his* **Gang.** *The* **Down and Outs** *change into more respectable clothes.*

BUGSY Right, Leroy, Babyface, you guys make sure you're hidden. Blousey, are you gonna get out of the way, else I'll have to take someone else to Hollywood.

BLOUSEY Sure, wisie.

He gives her two tickets.

BUGSY Two tickets to Hollywood.

BLOUSEY Oh, Bugsy!

She throws her arms around him. Suddenly **Babyface** *charges down the stairs.*

BABYFACE They're here, Bugsy! They're here!

BUGSY O.K. Everyone act like normal. Girls, off you go. Let's hear you. Music. Razamataz, hit the ivories!

The '**Customers**' *settle down and enjoy the show. The* **Girls** *sing and dance.*

Fat Sam's Grand Slam

> Anybody who is anybody
> Will soon walk through that door
> At Fat Sam's Grand Slam speakeasy
> Always able to find you a table
> There's room for just one more
> At Fat Sam's Grand Slam speakeasy
>
> *Once you get here
> Feel the good cheer
> Like they say in the poem

Fat Sam's ain't humble
But it's your home-sweet-home
Plans are made here
Games are played here
I could write me a book
Each night astounds you
Rumours are a-buzzing
Stories by the dozen
Look around you cousin
At the news we're making here
Anybody who is anybody
Will soon walk through that door
At Fat Sam's Grand Slam speakeasy

See the politician
Sitting by the kitchen
Said he caught his fingers
In the well he was wishing in

Repeat

Part of the way through the song **Dandy Dan's Gang** burst through the door at the top of **Fat Sam**'s office.

DANDY DAN   O.K. Everybody freeze!

The **Girls** scream. Everyone runs for cover.

FAT SAM   Bugsy. Guys. Let 'em have it!

Chaos breaks out. Splurge. Custard pies. Flour bombs. The entire company is involved. Above this pandemonium we hear the piano notes of the finale number, one voice to begin with, then all.

ALL

You Give a Little Love

We could have been anything that we wanted to be
And it's not too late to change
I'd be delighted to give it some thought
Maybe you'll agree that we really ought two . . . . .
      three . . . . . four

*We could have been anything that we wanted to be
Yes, that decision was ours
It's been decided we're weaker divided

Let friendship double-up our powers

We could have been anything that we wanted to be
And I'm not saying we should
But if we try it we'd learn to abide it
We could be the best at being good guys
Flowers of the earth
Who can even guess how much
A real friend is worth?
Good guys shake an open hand
Maybe we'll be trusting
If we try to understand
No doubt about it
It must be worth while
Good friends do tend to make you smile

*Repeat

**You give a little love
  And it all comes back to you
  You know you're gonna be remembered
  For the things that you say and do

**Repeat for as long as possible, on stage and off.

END

THE CHARACTERS

The following extracts are all taken from the book of the film and fill in some interesting details about the characters.

BUGSY MALONE

Bugsy wasn't the smartest guy in town but he had an air about him that was difficult to describe. A sort of inner dignity that didn't rely on crisp white cuffs and a diamond stick pin. He was no hood. He'd been around them, sure. He'd had his scrapes. And he generally came out on top. But he got a funny kind of pleasure just from being in the middle of things. Always there, but never involved. He'd been quite a useful boxer in his day, too. Except for one slight handicap. He had a jaw that had more glass in it than Macy's front window. But he still kept in trim. Made a few bucks — from 'this and that', he liked to say. In the main they were honest bucks — looking for promising fighters and steering them in the direction of Cagey Joe at Sluggers Gym.

He'd spent his life on the Lower East Side and it was a lot harder keeping on the straight and narrow than going crooked. With an Irish father and an Italian mother he had naturally grown up somewhat confused. He couldn't see his future as a spaghetti waiter in a restaurant or as a clerk at City hall, filling in endless forms. So he'd drifted from this to that. Never very crooked, not always completely honest. But generally to do with boxing, his great love.

BLOUSEY

Blousey Brown had always wanted to be famous. She got the bug very early — at the age of three she gave an impromptu recital for her family at Thanksgiving. She would tap dance a little and sing some, and what her rather squeaky voice lacked in volume she made up for with enthusiasm. Her audience was always especially encouraging. But what family doesn't have a talented child? In fact, there had been vaudeville acts in Blousey's family since way back. They hadn't gathered a great deal of fame amongst them — the yellowed notices in the cuttings book weren't too plentiful — but they were remembered with great affection. At Thanksgiving, when Blousey put on her shiny red tap shoes with the pink bows and did her annual turn, someone would say, 'She's got it all right. You can tell she's gonna be famous. There's a kind of sparkle in her eye. Bravo, Blousey. Bravo.'

It was the last 'Bravo' that did it. Since that moment, Blousey had been hooked on show business.

LEROY

A soft, cuddly teddy bear of a boy in a neighbourhood so tough you could get a Congressional medal for walking the streets after dark. But it hadn't spoiled Leroy. He smiled when he was provoked, and laughed when he was shouted at. There was a kindness from inside him that shone in his eyes and glittered from his pearly white teeth. Also, as they say in Louisiana, he was built like a brick chicken-house, and everyone knew that if you messed around too far with Leroy you were in danger of having the point of your chin punched somewhere back where your ears used to be.

FIZZY

Fizzy had whistled his bluesy song for as long as he could remember. He hadn't been taught it. He hadn't heard it on the radio and it wasn't anything Razamataz had played. It belonged to Fizzy. Whenever anyone asked him, 'What's that song you're whistling, Fizzy?' he used to shrug his shoulders. People used to think it meant he didn't know the title. It had no title — except for Fizzy's Tune. Fizzy wasn't the type to say 'It's a little number I composed myself' — people probably wouldn't have believed him. Fizzy was a janitor

and was meant to sweep up. That's how most people thought of him, because most people like to put folk in pigeon holes.

FAT SAM

Like most hoodlums, Fat Sam had clawed his way up from the streets to get a little recognition. A little notoriety. But whenever he ever made the papers or the newscasts it made him mad. Very mad.

'Alleged mobster king of the Lower East Side,' was it? There was no 'alleged' about it. Sam was king of these parts. There wasn't a racket or a shady deal in which he didn't have his fat podgy finger. No, there was no doubt. At least, not in Fat Sam's mind.

TALLULAH

She was the star of the show and everyone knew it. Her hair was a work of art, patiently created at Madame Monzani's Hair Parlour. She peered out from behind her curls with eyes that were wide open — but could narrow to a cool stare that cut guys in half. And often did. Tallulah was as cool as they come, and she pouted her red cupid-bow lips as she sang her songs in that ever-so-slinky way that drew besotted stares from the guys and envious looks from the girls. She was also Sam's girl, which made life a little easier for her and a little tougher for the rest of the girls. Not that Tallulah was without talent herself. She put over a number like no one else.

KNUCKLES

Fat Sam's number one man. He cracked his knuckles often, which is how he got his name. It always looked a little threatening as he idly clicked at the bones in his hands, but to tell the truth it was more nerves than bravado — though Knuckles never let on. He had a name to live up to and he was determined to do it.

SNAKE-EYES

Snake-Eyes got his name because of those two long ivory cubes that clicked and clicked away in his palm. He had been the king of any street corner crap game ever since he learned that a dice has six faces and a hood only needs two.

RITZY

Ritzy was the quietest of the bunch. He was a dapper dresser, with knife-edged creases down his trousers that could cut your throat. Ritzy was one of those people who always look like they've come straight from the laundry. He had starched eyelids, ears neatly pressed and steamed, and even his smile seemed to crease his face like it had been freshly applied by the best laundry in Chinatown.

LOUIS

Louis was called Louis because he resembled Shakedown Louis, a hero in these parts. No one ever knew Shakedown Louis, or what he did, but he had a name and it was enough for anyone that Louis resembled him. And anyway, whoever heard of a hoodlum called Joshuah Spleendecker. Mrs Spleendecker preferred Louis. And most of all Louis preferred Louis.

ANGELO

Angelo was called Angelo because his mother thought it was a cute name. It was also his father's name, and his grandfather's name, which meant that the chances of his being called Clarence or Albin were pretty slim.

DANDY DAN

Dandy Dan had devoted a lifetime to extravagant exhibitions of showy cool. His polo clothes were, of course, immaculate. After all, there were no errors in Dandy Dan's wardrobe. He chose his clothes with as much care as he used in choosing his tactics for outwitting Fat Sam.

BRONX CHARLIE

Bronx Charlie was the first to get out. He always sat up front with the driver, and when Dandy Dan wasn't around, Bronx Charlie was number one man in the gang.

DOODLE

For some reason, Doodle never seemed to fit in Dan's gang. He was one of those people who always look like they don't belong. Doodle was the black sheep of Dandy Dan's gang. His suit wasn't quite up to the tailored excellence of the other hoods'. He was a little crumpled around the places where the others boasted a knife-edge crease. It is true to say that he resembled a potato sack more than a tailor's dummy. He wore very thick glasses that perched, like the bottoms of milk bottles, on the end of his nose. The wire that held them together had pinched his nose for so many years that it had resulted in a permanent red mark across the bridge, and a rather squeaky nasal voice.

CAPTAIN SMOLSKY

The truth was that if Smolsky could make even one arrest they'd run
a headline in the Police Gazette proclaiming a miracle. Not that he
hadn't tried. He would read his detective manuals and the private
eye magazines from cover to cover, watch the movies – anything to
get a teeny, weeny inkling of how to track down his man, trap him,
arrest him and lock him in a cell. So far, sad to say, it hadn't worked.

O'DREARY

O'Dreary was the classic bronx flatfoot who had been promoted for
fear of what he might get up to if left alone to patrol the sidewalks.
Smolsky had suffered from insults enough as a kid and he enjoyed
getting his own back on anyone. O'Dreary was one of those
unfortunate people who was at the end of the line. All he could do to
get even was to put too many sugars in Smolsky's coffee, or too much
mustard on his hot dog. To most people, that wouldn't seem much, but
O'Dreary was a simple person and his pleasures came easy. Smolsky
liked to hit O'Dreary, but what he didn't know was that O'Dreary
didn't mind. If Smolsky had known that, it would have annoyed him
even more.

THE PRODUCTION

The suggestions which follow on set design, back projection and props, come from schools and amateur theatrical groups which have already staged the play — before the playscript was available. These suggestions reflect a high degree of ingenuity and inventiveness and also illustrate the scope which *Bugsy Malone* offers. There is no one right way of constructing the stage or manufacturing splurge guns etc. It is hoped that each new production of the play will throw up some new possibility.

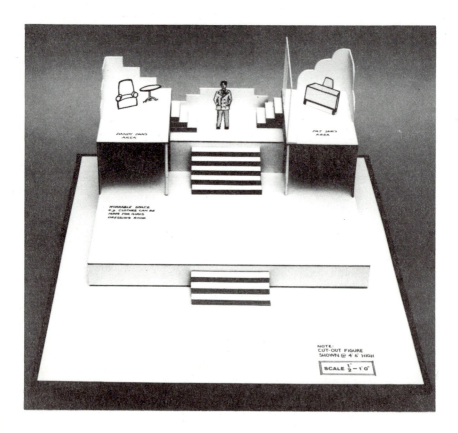

THE SET

'Staging the play was great fun. On the stage, behind the proscenium we built the two main sets, the Speakeasy and Fat Sam's office, on different levels. We also had a large gauze which came diagonally across the Speakeasy which was used for special effects on the cabaret stage, and was also used for projecting still slides of photographs (titles, newspapers etc.) Down the right hand side of the theatre we built a row of shops, starting with Pop Becker's and the bookcase entrance behind Sam's office to the Speakeasy, to Mama Lugini's, the Chinese Laundry and the drug-store. We used side-walk tables for the drug-store and the phone booth was stuck on the end of the row of shops. Bugsy used this phone, of course, but it was also used by Blousey to phone Fat Sam's and by Seymour Scoop to phone the City Desk. On the left hand side of the auditorium we built Dandy Dan's living room, and the warehouse. We had an orchestra pit for the small group of musicians and in between them and the audience, running across the theatre adjoining Dandy Dan's area with the street, we built a catwalk. We used the catwalk for the gymnasium, and the orchestra for the down-and-outs (very effective as they slowly went out of sight down the steps in the song).'

'Our production was staged in a small amateur theatre with limited facilities, therefore some design features evolved from simple problems of space, shape and size.

The fluid nature of action on stage and frequent changes of location led us to choose a fairly open set without curtains.

The "all-purpose" set was designed to accommodate an "office" from which Al and Lucy could intervene at ease in their narrator role;* an area for a small choir (balcony); band space (under and in front of office); and a screen. It also had to provide maximum floor area for dance/musical numbers etc. Major location changes were achieved by sections of the set being hinged (as in the bar, down left), pulled out from box sections (as in the thrust stage for the Speakeasy), by the addition of stage props (chairs/tables etc), and by props being flown in and out ('Speakeasy' or 'Sluggers Gym' signs, sedans etc). Minor locations were indicated by fairly extensive use of lighting and by slides/ciné film. Major locations included: Office (permanent); Street; Speakeasy; Sluggers Gym; Theatre; Cafe; Park.

The back-drop was a montage of '20s street signs, shop frontages etc. The artwork was designed to have maximum impact as the audience entered and, along with slides and music during the 30 minutes leading up to performance, lull the audience into the feel

*Two characters added to the play for this school's version: 'Ace reporter' Al, and his colleague Lucy, to whom he recounts the 'scoop' he's working on — 'Fat Sam v Dandy Dan'.

of the period before the cast even entered.

Secondly, and more importantly, it provided a direct background for street scenes (which often acted as dramatic links) so that by simply striking the accessories of other locations we created the street.'

'Our stage was Fat Sam's Speakeasy with two projections SR and SL for Sam and Dan's offices. These were permanent blocks and desks and props. The setting inside the bar was a typical bar with stairs CB for dance entrances and other entrances. Bar furniture was borrowed for tables and chairs. In front of curtains (closed) we acted street scenes and the soup kitchen. We kept everything simple but bright and shimmery as we needed space for dances.'

'The stage on which we performed was 3-4 feet high. At the back of that we placed the band and a bar at which we could seat the back-up singers. This left a large space in front for dancing, mobs and fights. Fat Sam's office and Dandy Dan's home could easily and quickly be brought in from either wing. A car which we had made and which was used in the street scene was left permanently in front of the main stage where we could also mass 120 down-and-outs!'

'Our school stage was the Speakeasy where we built a framework for Fat Sam's office. We built an apron stage in front of the school stage. We had Dan's hideout at another level to one side of the apron and used the apron for everything else!'

A SUGGESTED STAGE LAYOUT, COURTESY OF PINEWOOD STUDIOS

DESK

TELEPHONE

PAT SAM'S AREA

TELEPHONE BOX

SAFETY BARRIERS

BAND

SIDE TABLE

ARMCHAIR

DANDY DAN'S AREA

STAIRS UP TO STAGE

WORKABLE SPACE eg CLOTHES RAILS MAKE-UP TABLE DRESSING ROOM

SCALE: TO YOUR OWN JUDGEMENT

BACK PROJECTION

A line screen incorporated into the set allows for a greater flexibility in portraying different scenes, and increases the dramatic impact.

'Two projectors were used with a fade facility. The slides and films were an integral part of the show and had several functions. They enabled us:

1   to achieve effects not possible on stage (eg a ciné chase involving level crossing/train, etc.);
2   to comment on or heighten stage action or mood (eg added action of splurge shots in Speakeasy; mood shots of Blousey during 'Ordinary Fool');
3   to suggest the passage of time by use of sequences (eg Blousey and Bugsy during 'a drive in the country' scene);
4   to set locations or give information to the audience simply by use of captions or pictures, and to link scenes during stage blackout.'

'The film clichés which can be repeated on screen (the line of excited reporters — the spinning newspapers) cannot be done so easily on stage — so we compromised. We used black and white slides with the titles on and pictures from the twenties, and projected them during the singing of the title song. We also took photographs of the gang war, the three splurgings — the barber's shop, Mama Lugini's and Fingers Dobbs in bed, and projected them as Seymour Scoop phoned his report in to the city desk. We replaced some film clichés with stage clichés. For example, Blousey on a swing instead of on the river in a boat.'

PROPS

Splurge Guns

'Several ideas were tested in the pursuit of effective splurge guns, most of which resulted in the props designers being covered in foam. Originally we wanted to be able to 'lob' balls of splurge that would splatter the victim on impact. Thus our early designs were along the lines of ping-pong ball guns. The real problem here was creating a ball of splurge that would be able to withstand the pressure of being fired (and hold its shape) but which would be soft enough not to render large numbers of the cast unconscious. We tried various ideas including coating the splurge in sugar substance (rather like meringues), or encasing it in various paper balls. These ideas did not work. We eventually realised that a jet of splurge would be most effective and would probably involve the use of compressed air to fire it. An easy solution would have been to ensure the guns were always used near the wings, thus providing the opportunity of feeding the gun from a large (and powerful) splurge tank in the wings.

However, several staging considerations prevented this:

1 the splurge-firing gangsters had to be able to enter from many places (including the auditorium) with their guns;
2 it would have looked too contrived to always stand in the wings areas when splurging somebody;
3 although powerful splurge guns looked good in action, we had to be able to control the jet in order to avoid covering the set everytime they were used.

We realised then, that we had to have a totally portable splurge gun that was powerful enough to hit victims up to 2 metres away but not powerful enough to splurge the set (or audience). The final design was very effective and very, very simple.

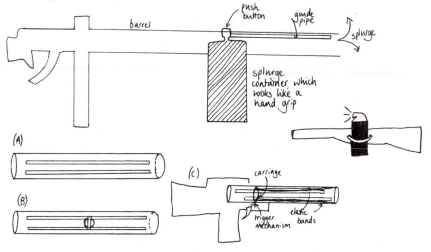

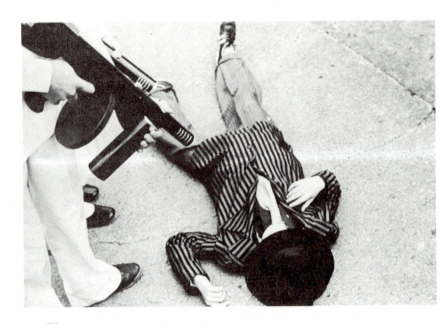

The guns were wooden with a pressurised container towards the front of the barrel (where the left hand-grip would normally be). The container was filled with splurge foam and pressurised by means of a simple foot pump before each act. The containers were operated by pressing a concealed button (situated on top of the barrel) with the left thumb.

It is worth mentioning that, in crowd scenes, we heightened the effect of the splurge by also using "splurge pies", having several "dummy" guns on stage, and by showing close-ups of people being splurged on screen.'

'The metalwork department made some machine-gun shaped pieces of wood with a metal holder into which we placed a tin of crazy-foam, painted black.'

'I considered it to be essential that at least some of the guns should fire some sort of "splurge". Firstly, therefore, we set about designing and then constructing a workable gun. This was finally achieved by using $2\frac{1}{2}''$ diameter plastic piping with two parallel grooves cut down opposite sides of the pipe, running the entire length, all but the last 2" either end. (A)

A carriage was then made, disc shaped, with a supporting bar fitted to the back which extended into the slits. (B)

Then the carriage was propelled by elastic bands, one either side, fixed to the mouth end of the pipe. A simple trigger mechanism was then fitted to a surround to make the gun look more realistic. (C)

The problems were:

1. they only had one shot and reloading was a tricky business which could only really be carried out off stage;
2. they were not very accurate;
3. they were limited in range — too strong elastic broke the carriages;
4. the splurge material itself took a long time to get right.

The splurge material proved to be more of a problem than the guns themselves. Firstly the splurge could not be allowed to stick to the sides of the barrels, but on impact it had to splatter. If it was too light it would not fly any distance; if it was too heavy the gun could not fire it.

Eventually we hit on a solution. A secret formula of a creamy substance was made — rather like whipped cream — and a measure was placed in a small square of thin, soft tissue paper. To aid the effectiveness of these guns we made a number of non-firing replicas from wood, had strobe lighting during the firing sequences and, perhaps most important of all, played a home-made tape-recorded sound effect of splurging squelches and guns firing over a public address system. For the battles, we found that flour bombs created a very good overall effect (loosely made tissue bombs which opened in flight or on impact). These were fine, except for the mess! Custard pies were made by cutting circles of foam rubber as the bases, applying crazy-foam and slightly dampening the whole thing to give it weight and "splatability".

'We found no method of producing the splurge guns as such. Instead we merely used a few "machine guns" and crazy foam in custard pie form: the audience (and cast) seemed quite happy with this nonsensical compromise.'

'Splurge guns were changed to small, pistol-sized guns, extended by tubing and with additions to look realistic. They were toys, bought from toy shops, which fire table-tennis balls. They were slightly unreliable and we lost a lot of balls! Quite effective though!'

Bike sedans

'During the scenes involving the sedans, a car frontage (or two cars) were flown in to a down centre position. These scenes also involved the use of slides and ciné. In one sequence, part of the gang chase was shown on film and these showed the sides of the sedans as well as the front. Another sequence involved a large screen being flown in behind the cars and a film of a road rapidly disappearing behind them was projected.'